W9-DBF-191

344.0793
Stu

2795
GUMDROP
6/15/06
6/15/06

PO# 01-7314
FY: 05/06

Students' Rights

Opposing Viewpoints®

Jamuna Carroll, *Book Editor*

Bruce Glassman, *Vice President*
Bonnie Szumski, *Publisher*
Helen Cothran, *Managing Editor*

OPPOSING
VIEWPOINTS®
SERIES

Ivy Tech Community College
Gary Campus Library
3400 Broadway
Gary, Indiana 46408

GREENHAVEN PRESS
An imprint of Thomson Gale, a part of The Thomson Corporation

EVM = X

THOMSON
™
GALE

Detroit • New York • San Francisco • San Diego • New Haven, Conn.
Waterville, Maine • London • Munich

3/150

© 2005 Thomson Gale, a part of The Thomson Corporation.

Thomson and Star Logo are trademarks and Gale and Greenhaven Press are registered trademarks used herein under license.

For more information, contact
Greenhaven Press
27500 Drake Rd.
Farmington Hills, MI 48331-3535
Or you can visit our Internet site at http://www.gale.com

ALL RIGHTS RESERVED.
No part of this work covered by the copyright hereon may be reproduced or used in any form or by any means—graphic, electronic, or mechanical, including photocopying, recording, taping, Web distribution or information storage retrieval systems—without the written permission of the publisher.

Every effort has been made to trace the owners of copyrighted material.

Cover credit: © AP Photo/The Wheeling News Register/John Wickline

LIBRARY OF CONGRESS CATALOGING-IN-PUBLICATION DATA
Students' rights / Jamuna Carroll, book editor.
p. cm. — (Opposing viewpoints series)
Includes bibliographical references and index.
ISBN 0-7377-3088-9 (lib. : alk. paper) — ISBN 0-7377-3089-7 (pbk. : alk. paper)
1. Students—Civil rights—United States. 2. Students—Legal status, laws,
etc.—United States. I. Carroll, Jamuna. II. Series.
KF4150.S78 2005
344.73'0793—dc22   2004059761

Printed in the United States of America

"Congress shall make no law. . . abridging the freedom of speech, or of the press."

First Amendment to the U.S. Constitution

The basic foundation of our democracy is the First Amendment guarantee of freedom of expression. The Opposing Viewpoints Series is dedicated to the concept of this basic freedom and the idea that it is more important to practice it than to enshrine it.

Contents

Why Consider Opposing Viewpoints?

*"The only way in which a human being can make some
approach to knowing the whole of a subject is by hearing
what can be said about it by persons of every variety of
opinion and studying all modes in which it can be looked
at by every character of mind. No wise man ever
acquired his wisdom in any mode but this."*

John Stuart Mill

In our media-intensive culture it is not difficult to find differing opinions. Thousands of newspapers and magazines and dozens of radio and television talk shows resound with differing points of view. The difficulty lies in deciding which opinion to agree with and which "experts" seem the most credible. The more inundated we become with differing opinions and claims, the more essential it is to hone critical reading and thinking skills to evaluate these ideas. Opposing Viewpoints books address this problem directly by presenting stimulating debates that can be used to enhance and teach these skills. The varied opinions contained in each book examine many different aspects of a single issue. While examining these conveniently edited opposing views, readers can develop critical thinking skills such as the ability to compare and contrast authors' credibility, facts, argumentation styles, use of persuasive techniques, and other stylistic tools. In short, the Opposing Viewpoints Series is an ideal way to attain the higher-level thinking and reading skills so essential in a culture of diverse and contradictory opinions.

In addition to providing a tool for critical thinking, Opposing Viewpoints books challenge readers to question their own strongly held opinions and assumptions. Most people form their opinions on the basis of upbringing, peer pressure, and personal, cultural, or professional bias. By reading carefully balanced opposing views, readers must directly confront new ideas as well as the opinions of those with whom they disagree. This is not to simplistically argue that everyone who reads opposing views will—or should—change his or her opinion. Instead, the series enhances readers' understanding of their own views by encouraging confrontation with opposing ideas. Careful examination of others' views can lead to the readers' understanding of the logical inconsistencies in their own opinions, perspective on why they hold an opinion, and the consideration of the possibility that their opinion requires further evaluation.

Evaluating Other Opinions

To ensure that this type of examination occurs, Opposing Viewpoints books present all types of opinions. Prominent spokespeople on different sides of each issue as well as well-known professionals from many disciplines challenge the reader. An additional goal of the series is to provide a forum for other, less known, or even unpopular viewpoints. The opinion of an ordinary person who has had to make the decision to cut off life support from a terminally ill relative, for example, may be just as valuable and provide just as much insight as a medical ethicist's professional opinion. The editors have two additional purposes in including these less known views. One, the editors encourage readers to respect others' opinions—even when not enhanced by professional credibility. It is only by reading or listening to and objectively evaluating others' ideas that one can determine whether they are worthy of consideration. Two, the inclusion of such viewpoints encourages the important critical thinking skill of objectively evaluating an author's credentials and bias. This evaluation will illuminate an author's reasons for taking a particular stance on an issue and will aid in readers' evaluation of the author's ideas.

It is our hope that these books will give readers a deeper understanding of the issues debated and an appreciation of the complexity of even seemingly simple issues when good and honest people disagree. This awareness is particularly important in a democratic society such as ours in which people enter into public debate to determine the common good. Those with whom one disagrees should not be regarded as enemies but rather as people whose views deserve careful examination and may shed light on one's own.

Thomas Jefferson once said that "difference of opinion leads to inquiry, and inquiry to truth." Jefferson, a broadly educated man, argued that "if a nation expects to be ignorant and free . . . it expects what never was and never will be." As individuals and as a nation, it is imperative that we consider the opinions of others and examine them with skill and discernment. The Opposing Viewpoints Series is intended to help readers achieve this goal.

David L. Bender and Bruno Leone,
Founders

Greenhaven Press anthologies primarily consist of previously published material taken from a variety of sources, including periodicals, books, scholarly journals, newspapers, government documents, and position papers from private and public organizations. These original sources are often edited for length and to ensure their accessibility for a young adult audience. The anthology editors also change the original titles of these works in order to clearly present the main thesis of each viewpoint and to explicitly indicate the opinion presented in the viewpoint. These alterations are made in consideration of both the reading and comprehension levels of a young adult audience. Every effort is made to ensure that Greenhaven Press accurately reflects the original intent of the authors included in this anthology.

Introduction

"[A] proper education environment requires close supervision of schoolchildren. . . . When children enter the schoolhouse gates, they submit themselves to the temporary custody and control of their teachers and administrators, and must abide by their rules."
—*U.S. Supreme Court*

"Does the process of denying civil rights to children succeed in creating a safer learning environment?"
—*Dave Kopel*

In Claremont High School's newspaper, the *Wolfpacket*, a special section on sex drew great controversy from students, administrators, and members of the community. *Wolfpacket* adviser Becca Feeney had encouraged student journalists to act on their idea to compose articles on abstinence, sex education, and masturbation. "It is important to cover things that are relevant, timely and important to the student population," she said. The students handled the issues maturely, but people were shocked that the articles covered such sensitive topics. Parents and community members wrote editorials to the local paper. Lawyers were called. Ultimately, the school principal decided, from that moment on, to review each issue of the *Wolfpacket* before it was printed. This practice, called prior review, is just one of many that generate heated debate over students' rights.

To prevent similar controversy, many schools routinely censor their newspapers. This practice is unnerving to some who feel that students have a right to express their opinions and learn about any topic pertaining to young people. These rights proponents argue that restricting speech violates students' rights to freedom of expression and freedom of the press. However, some administrators and parents disagree, citing the Supreme Court's acknowledgment that schools have a duty to maintain an orderly environment and protect students. To achieve these objectives, these analysts contend, schools must shield youth from inappropriate content. The Court further maintains that students in schools have fewer rights than do adults.

The Supreme Court has ruled that a school can limit student expression in a school-sponsored newspaper as long as there is reasonable educational justification. For instance, speech that is inconsistent with a school's "basic educational mission" can be restricted even though the government could not censor similar speech outside of school. As a result of the Court's ruling, discussions on teen parenting programs, safe sex, domestic violence, suicide, crime on campus, administrators' wrongdoing, and student drug and alcohol abuse have been censored in school publications. In *Hazelwood School District v. Kuhlmeier*, for instance, the Court found that a principal acted reasonably in removing stories from a high school newspaper about students' pregnancies, sexual activity, and use of birth control since he meant "to avoid the impression that [the school] endorses the sexual norms of the subjects."

Topics that have not been approached maturely are also subject to censorship. One article on sex was removed from the Plano Senior High School newspaper because it included slang like "get freaky." This action is constitutional, says the Court, because schools may censor that which is "ungrammatical, poorly written, inadequately researched, biased or prejudiced, vulgar or profane, or unsuitable for immature audiences." Other sensitive information, such as "the particulars of teenage sexual activity in a high school setting" and "speech that might reasonably be perceived to advocate drug or alcohol use, irresponsible sex, or conduct otherwise inconsistent with the 'shared values of a civilized social order,'" can also be restricted. Sometimes, school officials claim, censorship is also justified to protect students' privacy. In a small school or one where only a few students are pregnant, for example, anonymous quotes by a pregnant student can easily be attributed to that student. In such cases, some say, interviews with pregnant or otherwise identifiable students should not be printed.

Rights advocates, on the other hand, believe that a free press is advantageous for all students, providing an avenue by which they can express their opinions and channel their emotions through writing. Harry Proudfoot and Alan Weintraub of Westport High School state, "We'd rather have the ideas in print in the school newspaper where the students can learn to harness their energy, anger, and intensity, than in an underground publication where that emotional angst just feeds on itself and creates greater negativity in the long run."

Moreover, these commentators assert, instructing students, and student journalists in particular, about their rights is imperative. Tim Dorway, a former media adviser, maintains, "School communities, and I mean staff, students and parents, benefit from schools that provide *every* opportunity to practice First Amendment freedoms." Teaching students that their rights are not important and that uncommon ideas should be repressed discourages students from standing up for their beliefs and makes them lose faith in democracy, these analysts believe. As *Press Freedom in Practice* puts it, "Without an appreciation for both the obligation of journalists to report the truth and the right of all Americans to express views that many find unpopular, we have little hope of creating a citizenry that will defend and protect those rights as adults."

In addition, most media advisers say that allowing students to function without censorship teaches them journalistic responsibility, preparing them for the world outside of school. Proudfoot and Weintraub assert, "Every student [journalist in our school] understands that with his or her right to freedom of the press comes the responsibility to use those rights ethically."

The issues raised by school newspaper censorship are similar to those central to other arguments about students' rights. In all cases rights proponents argue that students' liberties should be preserved while administrators and parents maintain that restricting some freedoms is essential in order to ensure the safety and rights of all students. Authors in *Opposing Viewpoints: Students' Rights* examine this debate in the following chapters: Do All Youth Have Equal Access to a Quality Education? Are Schools Justified in Restricting Students' Expression? Should Schools Be Allowed to Infringe on Students' Right to Privacy? Do School Drug Policies Violate Students' Rights? As the controversy over student newspaper censorship makes clear, deciding what rights students have and when and if they should be infringed upon is highly contentious.

CHAPTER 1

Do All Youth Have Equal Access to a Quality Education?

Chapter Preface

The United States has spent $8 trillion on education in the fifty years since schools were desegregated. Even so, some citizens charge that not all youths have equal access to a quality education. Journalist Brad Heath contends that the quality of education a child receives depends mostly on where the student lives. He writes,

> In wealthy areas like Southfield and Birmingham [Michigan], schools spend more than $5,300 on basic instruction for each child, money that buys experienced teachers and newer books. Put the same student in New Haven or Detroit and they will get an education worth barely half that. They endure bigger classes and are . . . less prepared to meet . . . minimum standards in reading, writing and math.

Indeed, in poor schools lacking equipment, supplies, and books as well as the funds to attract highly qualified teachers, students may receive a substandard education, many critics maintain.

Many of these analysts contend that this unevenness in educational quality undermines one of America's most cherished rights: the right to a quality education. A hallmark of the United States, they say, is its promise to treat people equally regardless of race, gender, or economic background. One test of that equality is whether all children have the opportunity to attend good schools. Many people believe that low- and even moderate-income students do not. U.S. Secretary of Education Rod Paige confirms this notion: "We still have a two-tiered public education system. Some fortunate students receive a world-class education. But millions are mired in mediocrity, denied a high-quality education."

This discrepancy becomes especially evident at the college level, where the cost of education falls on students and their families, not the states. "People can't afford college because it costs too much," says fifteen-year-old Erica Mundy. College tuition rates support Mundy's assessment. According to the College Board, the average cost of a four-year private school is about $80,000 for four years. Four years at a public university costs roughly $20,000. These costs are prohibitive for many families.

To provide low-income students with easier access to college, the United States introduced the Higher Education Act of 1965, which authorized student financial assistance for postsecondary education. Upon signing the law, President Lyndon B. Johnson proclaimed, "A high school senior anywhere in this great land of ours can apply to any college or any university in any of the 50 states and not be turned away because his family is poor."

Since then the government has continued to increase aid to students. Today, the College Board notes that a record $105 billion in financial aid is available to students and their families, and almost 60 percent of undergraduate students receive financial aid. However, less of this assistance now comes in the form of grants and more is in the form of low-interest loans that must be repaid.

Despite the federal government's attempt to ensure equal access to higher education, low-income high school graduates with high unmet financial need are far less likely to attend a four-year college and far more likely not to attend college at all, says the 2002 report *Empty Promises, The Myth of College Access in America*. According to the report, 87 percent of high-income high school graduates enrolled in college after graduation as compared to only 53 percent of low-income high school seniors. Based on these findings, the Advisory Committee on Student Financial Assistance warns that the country is facing "a national access crisis."

The report's main premises echo Paige's assertion that "equality of opportunity must be more than just a statement of law; it must be a matter of fact." The viewpoints in this chapter address who should have access to America's educational institutions and financial aid as well as how that equality may be achieved.

"Democrats and Republicans have the same goal at heart when it comes to education: giving all children access to excellent schools."

The No Child Left Behind Act Protects the Right of All Students to Receive a Quality Education

Rod Paige

Public school students are receiving poor educations, argues Rod Paige in the following viewpoint. Of most concern are minority, low-income, and urban students, Paige asserts, because their performance on assessments is even worse than that of their peers. He believes that the achievement gap can be closed with the implementation of the No Child Left Behind Act, which was passed in 2002. By holding public schools accountable for student performance on standardized tests, the law enables schools to pinpoint achievement gaps and ensures that students receive a high-quality education regardless of their background, he contends. Rod Paige, a Republican, is U.S. secretary of education.

As you read, consider the following questions:

1. In Paige's contention, how has education reform "grown up" under the No Child Left Behind Act?
2. What evidence does the author provide for the persistent achievement gap between ethnic groups?
3. When do children fall prey to "the soft bigotry of low expectations," according to Paige?

Rod Paige, "An Overview of America's Education Agenda," *Phi Delta Kappan*, vol. 83, May 2002, pp. 708–13. Copyright © 2002 by Phi Delta Kappa International. Reproduced by permission.

Our task began on President [George W.] Bush's second day in office, when he unveiled his No Child Left Behind plan. This plan sought to change the culture of education by using the same principles of reform that had already shown results in Texas: accountability for results, local control and flexibility, expanded parental options, and doing what works according to scientific research. We faced a formidable challenge. According to the National Assessment of Educational Progress, most of the progress in student performance in reading and math was made during the 1970s. Little has improved in terms of student performance since 1980. And while science scores declined in the 1970s and improved during the 1980s, they too were flat throughout the 1990s.

While these problems were evident, many school boards were enmeshed in arguments over such topics as budgets and work rules. The system was focused on itself, not on students.

The President designed his No Child Left Behind plan to guide Congress in reauthorizing the Elementary and Secondary Education Act (ESEA), the legislation that defines the federal role in education. It is the most sweeping reform of the federal role in education since ESEA was passed in 1965....

Ensuring Equal Access to a Good Education

Before I got to Washington, I thought that Democrats adhered to entirely different ideals about education than Republicans did. To my surprise, I discovered that Democrats and Republicans have the same goal at heart when it comes to education: giving all children access to excellent schools. They may disagree on what is the best way to reach this goal, but they are always thinking about what is best for students.

Throughout the past year [2001], Sen. [Edward] Kennedy [D-Mass.] and Rep. [George] Miller [D-Calif.] worked well with their Republican counterparts, Sen. Judd Gregg (R-N.H.) and Rep. John Boehner (R-Ohio), to turn the principles of No Child Left Behind into law. The dialogue spurred progress. The year before, members of Congress had struggled over positioning in education reform as well as in many other issues. Mired in partisan politics, they failed to reauthorize ESEA. This time, even after the attacks of September 11 [2001], Congress did not abandon its resolve to produce a good education bill that would improve schools for all students. While many sharp differences needed resolution, the members and their staffs worked with White House and Education Department staffs with great determination through the summer and fall and through anthrax and evacuations. In December, they sent the President the No Child Left Behind Act, which he signed on 8 January 2002, ushering in a new era in American education.

The No Child Left Behind law heralds a major change in direction for American schools. A river that had wandered sluggishly east suddenly shifted and began to flow west. Everyone involved in education—teachers and administrators, students and parents, business and community leaders—will notice the change, and the more they understand it, the more it will help them. The new westward current will flow swiftly, and it will carry everyone along. Boats that had run aground or been snagged in the shallows will be shaken loose and brought back to midstream. Most important, the river and everyone on it will flow toward success.

No Child Left Behind helps us look at schools, governance, and the federal role in education in the right way. It reminds us that the goal of schools is not diplomas, but educated citizens. It assures us that the responsibility for student performance lies not just with educators, but also with communities. Most important, it changes the federal role in education from funding to investing. When federal spending becomes an investment, it gives the federal government leverage to demand results.

With the No Child Left Behind law, education reform has grown up. No longer is reform about access or money. No longer is it about compliance or excuses. Instead, it is about improving student achievement by improving the quality of the education we offer our students. It is once again focused on the student, not the system.

Rep. Miller summed it up well when he said, "This bill will help return our school system to the original goals of the 1965 Elementary and Secondary Education Act—to ensure that all children have an opportunity to learn regardless of income, background, or racial or ethnic identity. But unlike the laws on the books over the past 35 years, we will back up our commitment with a set of unambiguous expectations, time lines, and resources."

The Achievement Gap

There is no doubt that our system is in urgent need of repair. Half a century ago, had we known that America would make astonishing improvements in technology, put an end to government-enforced segregation, and spend more than $8 trillion on schools, we would have expected to finish the century with all our citizens—from business leaders to busboys—able to read, calculate, and understand American history. Instead, though our nation is blessed with many excellent schools and many excellent educators, our system is still failing too many children. According to the most recent National Assessment of Educational Progress (NAEP), only 32% of fourth-graders can read proficiently, and the proportion in urban areas is even lower. Twenty-six percent of urban fourth-graders are proficient readers, compared with 36% of suburban and 32% of rural fourth-graders. (If Americans in 1952 had known they would spend $8 trillion over 50 years, at the end of which time only about a third of children could read, they might have questioned that use of funds.)

There is also a persistent achievement gap between ethnic groups. While 40% of white fourth-graders read at or above the proficient level, only 12% of blacks and 16% of Hispanics perform as well. The situation is not better in high school. Our high school seniors scored lower on the 2000 NAEP math assessment than their predecessors in 1996. And, although more children are attending college, nearly a third of our college freshmen must take remedial courses. Minority students are taking more courses that will prepare them for college-level work. The performance of most minority groups is still measurably lower than that of whites, and an achievement gap between minority and disadvantaged students and their peers endures despite billions spent trying to close it.

Holding Schools Accountable

In order to eliminate the achievement gap and improve student performance across the board, we must hold educators

The No Child Left Behind Act Will Close Education Gaps

The new ESEA [Elementary and Secondary Education Act] is built on the foundation of its precursor, which was adopted in 1994. . . .

The new law [reauthorized by the No Child Left Behind Act] does include several important improvements over the old law:

- expands the information that must be provided to parents and reported to the public, including information about achievement gaps and teacher quality;
- strengthens the requirement that schools identified as needing improvement actually develop and implement plans to improve; and,
- requires, for the first time in the history of federal education legislation, every state to define what constitutes a qualified teacher and to ensure that schools educating low-income and minority students don't employ a disproportionate number of unqualified, inexperienced, or out-of-field teachers.

Together, these requirements should help to bring about much-needed public discussion—and much-needed change—in communities where achievement gaps between groups of students have not been addressed. . . .

The data clearly and consistently show that schools educating the highest proportion of low-income and minority students continue to employ a disproportionate number of unqualified, inexperienced, and out-of-field teachers, offer the least rigorous curriculum to their students, and get less than their fair share of money and other resources. Yet to this point, nobody has insisted that states find ways to assure that all students get the kind of educational opportunities they need to reach state standards.

The Education Trust, *ESEA: Myths Versus Realities*. www.edtrust.org.

---

accountable to the bold proposition that every child can learn. This is a belief that President Bush takes very seriously, and he means *no child* left behind quite literally. He does not mean that, after you siphon off the children who have disabilities, or were never properly taught how to read, or never learned English, or disrupted their classrooms, then the rest can learn. He means that all of our students, even the ones our system calls "hard to teach," can learn.

There is no middle ground or room for excuses. Either educators believe that every child can learn, or they do not. When educators begin to make excuses for children based on race or socioeconomics, both those who make excuses and our children fall prey to what the President calls "the soft bigotry of low expectations."

The No Child Left Behind law places accountability squarely in the center of our education system. The law requires each state to enact a strong accountability structure based on clear and high standards and a system of annual assessments to measure student progress against those standards.

Testing is not designed to punish students or teachers; it is an integral part of determining whether or not students are learning what the state has decided they should know. When we have clear standards and tests that are aligned to them, testing allows us to make sure every child is making progress. Annual testing allows us to identify and correct problems quickly, so that schools can be held accountable for the progress of their students. For this reason, the No Child Left Behind law calls for states to test their students annually in grades 3 through 8 in the basic subjects of reading and math. Science assessments will be less frequent, but no less important in tracking student progress. Students should make substantial progress every year, in every class, and annual assessments will ensure that they do. Every time they do not, we are not just wasting time, money, and opportunities; we are making students more discouraged, despondent, and disenfranchised.

Improving Student Performance

Every child's education should be a voyage of discovery, and the No Child Left Behind law is all about discovering and disseminating the information about student performance that assessments will provide. Test scores will be disaggregated by poverty, race, ethnicity, disability, and English proficiency so that we can see where the achievement gap exists and attack it so that no group is neglected. School districts and schools that fail to make adequate progress toward statewide goals will be identified for improvement and, over time, will be subject to corrective action and restructuring measures aimed at getting them back on course to meet state standards. Schools that meet or exceed adequate yearly progress objectives or close achievement gaps will be eligible for State Academic Achievement Awards.

Teachers will be able to use individual student data to tailor their teaching to the specific needs of each student. Principals will be able to use the data to make informed decisions about what their schools need in order to improve student performance. Parents will no longer wonder whether or not their children's schools are teaching them.

"The political agenda that produced NCLB ignores—or even promotes—inequality."

The No Child Left Behind Act Does Not Protect the Right of All Students to Receive a Quality Education

Stan Karp

In the following viewpoint Stan Karp charges that the No Child Left Behind (NCLB) Act, which imposes sanctions on schools that do not meet set standards, harms students and promotes inequality. By relying on undependable standardized testing and requiring schools to meet ridiculously high goals, the law sets up schools to fail, he asserts, harming poor students the most. NCLB also pushes struggling students out of school and leads schools to lower their standards, he claims. Stan Karp is a high school teacher and editor of *Rethinking Schools*, which encourages public school reform.

As you read, consider the following questions:

1. What does the author say about the mandate that No Child Left Behind imposes on schools to eliminate test score inequalities within twelve years?
2. Name four negative effects of mandatory standards and tests, as cited by Karp.
3. What is the author's objection to counting only the number of students who score above the passing level on a state test?

Stan Karp, speech at a Portland Area Rethinking Schools meeting, November 7, 2003. Copyright © 2003 by Stan Karp. Reproduced by permission.

The NCLB [No Child Left Behind] Act will not deliver on its promises to close the academic achievement gaps among groups of students, or bring school improvement to low performing schools, or assure that every child has a high quality teacher.

Now let me say at the outset that these are all worthy goals. Who would oppose a federal pledge to "Leave No Child Behind"? Who opposes the idea that all kids should receive a high quality education from a well-prepared teacher and that schools should be accountable for serving all children?

One of the problems we have in responding to this law is that it comes couched in high-sounding rhetoric that appeals to everyone who cares about schools and kids. And if you raise your voice and say, wait a minute this sounds nice, but the real impact this law is going to have in schools will not achieve any of these wonderful goals but instead is going to seriously damage one of the most important democratic institutions we have, then you need to be prepared to do a lot of explaining . . . and I'm going to try to do some of that today. . . .

NCLB Is a Hoax

We need to look behind the rhetoric we hear from our political leaders and the information we get from the media to discover the real agendas at work in our country's public policy and political life.

If you do look behind the rhetoric, you'll find many reasons why NCLB is a fraud that will leave many children behind and may in fact leave no public school standing. I'm going to lay out . . . my reasons first, just to give an indication of the many issues NCLB raises, most of them poorly, and then, focus on a couple of what I think are the most important issues. . . .

Here's why I think NCLB is a hoax:

1. The massive increase in testing that NCLB will impose on schools will hurt their educational performance, not improve it.
2. The funding for NCLB does not come anywhere near the levels that would be needed to reach even the narrow and dubious goal of producing 100% passing rates on state tests for all students by 2014.

3. The mandate that NCLB imposes on schools to eliminate inequality in test scores among all student groups
within 12 years is a mandate that is placed on no other
social institution, and reflects the hypocrisy at the heart
of the law.

4. The sanctions that NCLB imposes on schools that
don't meet its test score targets will hurt poor schools
and poor communities most.

5. The transfer and choice provisions of NCLB[1] will create chaos and produce greater inequality within the
public system without increasing the capacity of receiving schools to deliver better educational services. . . .

Standards and Tests Are Poor Substitutes for Education

The standards and testing regime holds out no hope of solving the problems it pretends to document. Many of us know
that standards and tests offer a kind of counterfeit accountability, one that sorts and labels kids on the basis of multiple
choice questions as a substitute for educating them. Mandating standards and tests is also a substitute for the much more
difficult and costly process of real school improvement. Ex-
ternally imposed standards and tests do virtually nothing to
increase the capacity of schools to deliver better educational
services. They also generally impose high-stakes consequences on the victims of educational failure rather than on
those responsible for it. For all the talk about "accountability," there is no accountability in this new law for the politicians who are imposing large measures of ill-conceived and
counterproductive administrative and budgetary chaos on
schools and local districts.

Still we do need to find more effective ways to show to
parents and communities how the narrow misuse of standards and tests can make things worse instead of better for
their kids and their schools. When tests are used to make
high stakes decisions about whether kids get promoted or
graduate, or whether schools lose funding, or teachers lose
their jobs, they narrow the focus of what teachers do in class-

1. The NCLB Act allows students to leave schools that do not meet standards.

rooms and limit the ability of schools to serve the broader needs of children and their communities.

High-stakes tests push struggling students out of school; they promote tracking [of teachers' credentials]; they encourage schools to adopt inappropriate practices for young children, children with special needs and English language learners. Overuse of testing encourages cheating scandals, and makes schools and students vulnerable to inaccurate and, at times, corrupt practices by commercial testing firms. On top of all that, standardized tests are scientifically unreliable and provide little real useful information about the learning needs of students.

NCLB Sets Schools Up to Fail

In the past two decades, most states and districts have already dramatically increased the use of standardized tests without solving the problems of poor schools. Quite the opposite, they have turned many schools into "dittolands" where dismal test prep drives the curriculum. Now some estimates are that the new federal law will require states to give more than 200 additional tests on top of what they're already using.

As many of you know, NCLB requires states to give annual tests in reading and math in grades 3–8 and at least once in high school. Additional annual tests are mandated in science beginning in 2007. . . .

The key to school improvement is not standards and tests, but teachers and students. And while those teachers and students need a complicated mix of support, resources, motivation, pressure, leadership and professional skills to succeed, the idea that this mixture can be provided by standards and tests is simply wrong, and is not supported by any educational research or real world experience.

The AYP [Adequate Yearly Progress] formulas in the new federal law are the latest example of just how damaging this approach can be. They simply set schools up to fail, including largely successful ones. They seem designed to demoralize educators and create a widespread public perception of systemic failure that will erode the common ground that a universal system of public education needs to survive. The AYP formulas also invest a ridiculous power in an extremely unreliable measure—year-to-year changes in standardized test scores. Under AYP each school is judged by a matrix of 40 indicators tied to state test scores. Maybe you've seen the charts. There are ten student groups: total population, special education students, English language learners, white, African-American, Asian/Pacific Islander, Native American, Hispanic, other ethnicities, and economically disadvantaged. (Interestingly, there is no gender break down.) In each category there are two mandates: 95% of kids in each group must take the state assessment, and each group must make its AYP target, which is the increment needed to bring all students in every group to 100% passing by 2014. Any school that misses even one of these targets for two consecutive years gets put on the needs improvement list and is supposed to start permitting student transfers. Three years brings corrective action and supplemental tutorial services; four years brings reconstitution, including replacement of school staff; five years brings restructuring, which can mean anything from state takeover to imposing private management on public schools. . . .

Schools Are Lowering Their Standards

[One] way states are responding to NCLB is by lowering their standards to avoid sanctions. For example, last year [2002] when the list of failing schools came out—excuse me, I should say the lists of schools in need of improvement but which are generally reported in the local paper as failing schools—Michigan had the most, over 1,500. Arkansas and Wyoming had none. So Michigan lowered the percentages of students who had to pass to get a school off the list, for example dropping the required passing rate on the high school English test from 75% to 42%. That reduced the number of schools needing improvement to 216.

Colorado decided to lump students previously characterized as "partially proficient" with those called "proficient."

In Texas, the supposed model for the Bush education plan, the Texas State Board was so horrified at the poor performance on the new third grade reading test, they voted to reduce the number of correct answers students needed so fewer schools would miss their AYP targets.

This is the kind of school improvement you can expect

from AYP. First huge areas of schooling are excluded completely from what is tested, and then statistical game-playing manipulates what's left.

The Public Is Uninformed About NCLB

Unfortunately so far the public has only a vague idea of any of this. A Gallup poll conducted this summer found that

'EDUCATION IS THE ONLY WAY UP, KIDS'

POOR SCHOOL DISTRICTS

RICH SCHOOL DISTRICTS

Engelhardt. © 1993 by Thomas Engelhardt in the *St. Louis Post-Dispatch*. Reproduced by permission of the cartoonist.

76% of those surveyed knew "very little" or "nothing" about the new law. The poll director told *Education Week* that "It is an uninformed public on No Child Left Behind."

Not surprisingly, a large majority of those polled agreed with the rhetorical goals of the legislation. Again, who would oppose a federal pledge to "Leave No Child Behind"? Over seventy percent also said it was very important to close achievement gaps between students from different racial, ethnic, and class backgrounds.

But according to *Education Week*, when they were told about the actual testing and accountability provisions of the law, "the public disagreed with some of the core elements. . . ."

For example, under AYP the only thing that counts is the number of students who score above the passing level on the state test. So on a test like New Jersey's High School Proficiency Assessment, where a passing score is 200, helping a bilingual, special education student from a low income household raise his/her test score from, say, a 50 to 199 counts for nothing, and in fact counts as a failure in four different subgroups. Moving a student from 199 to 200 is success.

According to the Gallup poll, when the public is given these kinds of details, people opposed such practices. Eighty-four percent said "a better way to judge the job a public school is doing would be to determine whether students show 'reasonable improvement from where they started.' Sixty-six percent, also said a single statewide test would not provide a fair picture of whether a public school is in need of improvement."

In other words, the public broadly supports the idea that federal policy should help reduce inequality in education, but is largely uninformed about how NCLB purports to do this. We need to let them know.

NCLB Promotes Inequality

But this "information gap" between public support for reducing educational inequality and widespread ignorance about the specific impact NCLB will have on schools is a reflection of a much deeper contradiction at the heart of the new law.

The new federal law imposes a mandate on schools that is

imposed on no other institution in society. Imagine a federal law that declared that 100% of all citizens must have adequate health care in twelve years or sanctions will be imposed on doctors and hospitals. Or all crime must be eliminated in twelve years or the local police department will face privatization.

The political agenda that produced NCLB ignores—or even promotes—inequality in virtually every area of society. Politicians like President [George W.] Bush posture about the "soft bigotry of low expectations." But the real measure of their concern is what they propose to do about such inequality, not only in schools, but in society at large, and here the record leaves little room for doubt: inequality is as American as processed apple pie.

Take, for example, income inequality among some of the same groups NCLB says must reach 100% test score equality within 12 years. Lots of research has established a strong link between student performance on standardized tests and family income. And while income inequality in a community is no excuse for school failure, certainly any serious federal plan to close the achievement gap in school needs to concern itself with trends in closely related areas like the resources that families and schools have to work with.

But a look at data on income inequality—especially through the prism of AYP—reveals the hypocrisy at the heart of the NCLB legislation. In 1991 the median household income for black families was about 58% of white income, Hispanic income was about 70%. If we applied the "logic" of AYP to this key measure of how our economy works, income gaps for blacks would need to narrow by 3.5% each year to pull even within twelve years, the same time frame schools have been given to equalize test scores. Hispanics, starting with a smaller gap, would have had to close the gap by 2.5% annually.

If you compare this to how the economy actually performed between 1991 and 2002, a period of supposedly unprecedented economic boom and growth, you'll find the U.S. economy would not have met its AYP targets for income inequality for any year for either group. At the end of twelve years, the gap between black and white income had narrowed only a pitiful 3.7%; for Hispanics the gap was just .4% less than it was in 1991.

If we lived in an alternate universe where income equality really was a goal of federal economic policy and an NCLB-like system of sanctions put pressure on the titans of industry and commerce to attain such a lofty goal, what do you think might be appropriate remedies for such a dismal performance: "corrective action" to borrow the language of NCLB sanctions? Economic "restructuring"? "Reconstitution" of our major corporations? How about "state takeover"?

The point, of course, is that there is no relevant area of social policy, from household income to child poverty rates to health care coverage to school spending, where federal policy currently mandates equality among all population groups within twelve years under threat of sanctions—except standardized test scores in public schools. If this sounds unfair and absurd, it's because it is. It's a plan to use achievement gaps to label schools as failures, without providing the support, resources and strategies needed to overcome them.

"Eliminating affirmative action is re-segregating higher education."

Affirmative Action in College Admissions Ensures Equality

Graciela Elizabeth Geyer, interviewed by Nic Paget-Clarke

In the following viewpoint, originally an interview by *In Motion Magazine's* Nic Paget-Clarke, Graciela Elizabeth Geyer of the United States Student Association argues that affirmative action policies promote equality. These policies, in which colleges consider race in admissions, ensure that minorities have an equal opportunity to attend college, she asserts. Because discrimination is pervasive in the admissions process, claims Geyer, race must be considered in admissions. Believing that affirmative action is an effective response to racism, Geyer maintains that eliminating affirmative action creates a hostile environment and segregates colleges. Graciela Elizabeth Geyer is the director of the Student of Color Campus Diversity Project. *In Motion Magazine* is an online U.S. publication about democracy.

As you read, consider the following questions:
1. According to Geyer, how did legislators help to repeal SP1 and SP2?
2. What two examples does the author provide as evidence that racism is institutionalized in college admissions?
3. What is Geyer's stated objection to the term "racial preferences"?

Nic Paget-Clarke and Graciela Elizabeth Geyer, "Eliminating Affirmative Action Is Re-Segregating Higher Education," *In Motion Magazine*, July 2, 2001. Copyright © 2001 by NPC Productions. Reproduced by permission.

In Motion Magazine: Please give me an update on affirmative action in California [and] Michigan?

Graciela Elizabeth Geyer: [In May 2001] the University of California (UC) regents, under pressure from student and community groups, finally repealed Standing Policies (SP) 1 and 2. SP1 and SP2 were initiated in 1995 under the direction of Governor Pete Wilson and UC Regent Ward Connerly to eliminate affirmative action in admissions and hiring at the University of California. They were a catalyst in pushing the anti-affirmative action Proposition 209 which was passed in the fall of 1996 by ballot initiative.

Even though the repeal of SP1 and SP2 does not allow the university to use race and gender in admissions and hiring decisions because Proposition 209 is still in place, organizing their repeal has been a student campaign since 1995. The repeal is seen as the first step in acknowledging the damage that 209 has done to the University of California.

Strong Support for Affirmative Action

The repeal itself was really exciting. I was there at the regents meeting in San Francisco and I would say about 250 students and community members turned up. It was great to see alumni come to the meeting and speak about the fact that without affirmative action they would not have been accepted into UC Berkeley Law for example. The other great thing was the incredible support in the legislature for affirmative action. Many legislators came to the Regents meeting, most of them UC alumni themselves, and brokered a deal the night of the meeting to re-write weak language, making a strong statement to repeal the policy. Until then, Ward Connerly and a few other regents had succeeded in watering it down and had the support to pass that version.

The point the legislators brought home was that many of their constituents, taxpayers, have been effectively shut out of the UC system. The state is now over half people of color. Legislators of color acknowledged that affirmative action was the reason they had the opportunity to attend the UC, and are now able to give back to their communities. Ironically, some of the most conservative regents made statements of support. One commented that his daughter at

Boalt Law [Berkeley] had mentioned to him that her "minority" friends had expressed that the UC was a hostile environment for them because of SP1 and 2.

Unfortunately, the repeals were not well covered in the national news. They were covered fairly well in California but you didn't hear much about them anywhere else.

In Michigan, they are still in the process of hearing an appeal to a Michigan law school case in which the use of race in admissions was ruled unconstitutional. Two separate judges heard undergraduate and graduate law school cases. The undergraduate case resulted in a positive ruling. The judge permitted use of race in admissions stating that the university had proved diversity was a "compelling interest" in education which merited using race and gender in affirmative action in admissions. The judge in the law school case ruled that there was no compelling interest—even though the judges are in the same circuit. Both cases are being appealed up through the courts and haven't quite made it to the Supreme Court yet.[1] . . .

Unfortunately, the case in Michigan [*Grutter v. Bollinger*] focuses solely on diversity's importance to the learning environment and doesn't address the fact that affirmative action is necessary to combat and to prevent discrimination.

The Significance of the SP1 and SP2 Repeals

Why are the California repeals important?

Graciela Elizabeth Geyer: Enrolling a diverse class is made up of three steps: getting a diverse applicant pool, accepting a diverse class, and getting those students who have been accepted to enroll. Eliminating affirmative action has impacted all of these rates. The repeal was increasingly important to the regents because on top of the high drop in the acceptance rate, in the past five years students of color who were accepted to the UC were choosing to enroll at lower rates as well. Students and community have found that the university has become a hostile environment.

---

1. The judges in the undergraduate case, *Gratz v. Bollinger*, determined in 2003 that race-based admissions are unconstitutional. The *Grutter v. Bollinger* decision, also in 2003, upheld race-conscious admissions.

The repeal is also significant because the regents unanimously voted to repeal this policy. A variety of regents made statements such as, "We see the damage that it has done," and "We don't want to be a party to it". It has put the university admissions process in the spotlight and the legislature is getting involved in examining the process and pushing the university to publicly examine what exactly has happened to the admissions process.

Institutionalized Racism

What are the barriers in the admissions process to students of color and under-represented students? For example, there has been research, and even a lawsuit, regarding discriminatory admissions policies such as the over-use of the SAT because without consideration of race (or other disadvantage), the SAT can prevent students that would otherwise be successful from entering the university.

Affirmative Action Fights Discrimination

Affirmative action means taking positive steps to end discrimination, to prevent its recurrence, and to create new opportunities that were previously denied qualified minorities and women.

President Lyndon Johnson explained the rationale behind the contemporary use of affirmative action to achieve equal opportunity in a 1965 speech: "You do not take a person, who for years, has been hobbled by chains and liberate him, bring him up to the starting line of a race and then say 'you are free to compete with all the others,' and still believe that you have been completely fair."

The debate over affirmative action carries enormous implications for the lives of women and people of color, since such programs have created opportunities too long denied them.

"Affirmative Action," Civilrights.org, 2002.

In addition, the university uses college-weighted GPAs for honors and advanced placement (AP) classes [which can boost GPA] that are not equally available to all California students. A very small percent, 4 or 5 %, of students of California schools have up to 10 AP classes available for which they can get extra credit. On the other hand, 40% of California students have one or no classes that are available to them at their school.

These are just two examples of how racism is institutionalized in admissions and requires the consideration of race until race is no longer a significant factor in educational opportunity prior to college admissions. Because educational opportunity is not distributed in a "race neutral" manner, we need to consider race in admissions. . . .

Since affirmative action has been battled over for about 40 years now, do the terms mean the same? When people say affirmative action is quotas and set-asides [positions guaranteed to minorities], how do you respond to that?

Graciela Elizabeth Geyer: Legally, affirmative action cannot be quotas. The [*University of California Regents v.*] *Bakke* decision [in 1978] ruled, 5-4, that quotas were illegal and there can be no program where white students can not also compete. In terms of admissions, there are no set-asides. Set-asides is a term used in contracting.

There are no quotas or set-asides used in implementing affirmative action in admissions. "Racial preferences," another term coined by the Right, assumes that there are not already "racial preferences," for white people throughout our society that require a positive inclusion of people of color such as affirmative action does. But definitions are the crux of the problem. Because of the incredible amount of resources that conservative foundations and organizations have had to flood the media with their definition of affirmative action, the media regularly interchanges affirmative action and racial preferences.

Re-Segregating Our Society

Eliminating affirmative action is re-segregating higher education. When you get the "we may have needed it in the past but we live in a color-blind [era now] . . ." tell them there are still states the federal government has not yet declared desegregated in education. Affirmative action is a response to institutionalized discrimination. The Right has been able to weasel out of being responsible for that by talking about it on an isolated and individual level. But if we look at the numbers of undergraduate admissions and graduation, and beyond that, the number of lawyers and doctors in society that are of color, and we look at California and Texas—the two public universities that graduate the largest number of Chicano lawyers and Black lawyers outside of historically Black colleges, we quickly realize eliminating affirmative action will effectively wipe out the small number of doctors and lawyers and other professionals of color in the U.S. Eliminating affirmative action is not just about resegregating higher education—it's about re-segregating our society in general.

When we already have so much residential and occupational segregation, eliminating affirmative action aggravates the situation. I think that a lot of universities are worried about this and a lot of state legislators are worried about this. Particularly in states that are very diverse. When you have a public education system where more than 50% of the state is of color, then how are you going to respond to the voters, the changing demographics. The reason why the legislature was so involved in California is because of pressure from the community of not-served and under-served, their constituents.

If we don't consider race and gender in the admissions process then we are saying that people have equal opportunity regardless of race and gender and that is just not true. That's what we need to start talking about.

"Quota systems that use race to include or exclude people from higher education . . . are divisive, unfair and impossible to square with the Constitution."

Affirmative Action in College Admissions Is Discrimination

George W. Bush

In the following viewpoint George W. Bush asserts that college admissions programs that award bonus points to minority students based solely on their race are unfair and unconstitutional. Prejudiced policies that accept or reject students because of the color of their skin cannot effectively combat racism, he contends. While Bush concedes that not enough minorities attend college and that schools should seek diversity, he believes that fairer methods can be used to ensure a diverse student body. George W. Bush is the forty-third president of the United States.

As you read, consider the following questions:
1. According to Bush, what should a college education teach?
2. Under the University of Michigan's admissions program, which students receive twenty bonus points and why, in Bush's contention?
3. How can colleges diversify their student bodies, according to Bush?

George W. Bush, speech given in the Roosevelt Room, Washington, DC, January 15, 2003.

The Supreme Court will soon hear arguments in a case [*Gratz v. Bollinger*] about admission policies and student diversity in public universities. I strongly support diversity of all kinds, including racial diversity in higher education. But the method used by the University of Michigan to achieve this important goal is fundamentally flawed.

At their core, the Michigan policies amount to a quota system that unfairly rewards or penalizes prospective students, based solely on their race. So, tomorrow my administration will file a brief with the court arguing that the University of Michigan's admissions policies, which award students a significant number of extra points based solely on their race, and establishes numerical targets for incoming minority students, are unconstitutional.

Discriminatory Policies Do Not Combat Prejudice

Our Constitution makes it clear that people of all races must be treated equally under the law. Yet we know that our society has not fully achieved that ideal. Racial prejudice is a reality in America. It hurts many of our citizens. As a nation, as a government, as individuals, we must be vigilant in responding to prejudice wherever we find it. Yet, as we work to address the wrong of racial prejudice, we must not use means that create another wrong, and thus perpetuate our divisions.

America is a diverse country, racially, economically, and ethnically. And our institutions of higher education should reflect our diversity. A college education should teach respect and understanding and goodwill. And these values are strengthened when students live and learn with people from many backgrounds. Yet quota systems that use race to include or exclude people from higher education and the opportunities it offers are divisive, unfair and impossible to square with the Constitution.

In the programs under review by the Supreme Court, the University of Michigan has established an admissions process based on race.[1] At the undergraduate level, African American

1. In June 2003 the Supreme Court found the process to be unconstitutional.

The Troubling Practice of Racial Profiling

Known euphemistically as "affirmative action" and practiced by virtually every selective university in the nation, racial preferences mean that minority applicants are evaluated under a different, typically lower, standard than that applied to nonminority candidates. In recent years, such dual-admissions systems have been deemed unconstitutional by federal courts in Texas, Michigan, and Georgia. . . .

Slogans like "diversity" and "affirmative action" can't hide the fact that many of our nation's universities engage in a form of racial profiling—that is, selecting people based primarily on the color of their skin. We should be deeply troubled when the police do it. So too should we be troubled when admissions officers engage in the practice. Classifying and selecting people based on race—no matter how beneficent the professed motive is—undermines a vital moral and constitutional principle, namely, that people should be judged as individuals, without regard to their race.

Curt A. Levey, *National Review Online*, June 11, 2001. www.national review.com.

---

students and some Hispanic students and Native American students receive 20 points out of a maximum of 150, not because of any academic achievement or life experience, but solely because they are African American, Hispanic or Native American.

To put this in perspective, a perfect SAT score is worth only 12 points in the Michigan system. Students who accumulate 100 points are generally admitted, so these 20 points awarded solely based on race are often the decisive factor.

At the law school, some minority students are admitted to meet percentage targets while other applicants with higher grades and better scores are passed over.[2] This means that students are being selected or rejected based primarily on the color of their skin. The motivation for such an admissions policy may be very good, but its result is discrimination and that discrimination is wrong.

Some states are using innovative ways to diversify their student bodies. Recent history has proven that diversity can

2. In 2003 in *Grutter v. Bollinger*, the Supreme Court upheld the university's graduate admissions process.

be achieved without using quotas. Systems in California and Florida and Texas have proven that by guaranteeing admissions to the top students from high schools throughout the state, including low income neighborhoods, colleges can attain broad racial diversity. In these states, race-neutral admissions policies have resulted in levels of minority attendance for incoming students that are close to, and in some instances slightly surpass, those under the old race-based approach.

Creating Diverse Campuses

We should not be satisfied with the current numbers of minorities on America's college campuses. Much progress has been made; much more is needed. University officials have the responsibility and the obligation to make a serious, effective effort to reach out to students from all walks of life, without falling back on unconstitutional quotas. Schools should seek diversity by considering a broad range of factors in admissions, including a student's potential and life experiences.

Our government must work to make college more affordable for students who come from economically disadvantaged homes. And because we're committed to racial justice, we must make sure that America's public schools offer a quality education to every child from every background, which is the central purpose of the education reforms I signed [in 2002].

America's long experience with the segregation we have put behind us and the racial discrimination we still struggle to overcome requires a special effort to make real the promise of equal opportunity for all. My administration will continue to actively promote diversity and opportunity in every way that the law permits.

*"These young [undocumented immigrants]
deserve a fresh start, both in fairness to
them and in our national interest."*

Subsidizing College Tuition for Illegal Immigrants Is Just

American Civil Liberties Union of Southern California

In the following viewpoint the American Civil Liberties Union of Southern California (ACLU/SC) contends that children of illegal immigrants should receive college tuition discounts. Under current law, these students pay high out-of-state tuition rates even if they live in-state, the organization claims. It is unfair to deny them access to affordable higher education simply because their parents illegally brought them to America, the ACLU/SC maintains. Making them eligible for financial aid and discounts, the organization predicts, would reduce dropout rates, increase tax revenue, and encourage students to give back to their communities. The ACLU/SC, founded in 1923 by writer and activist Upton Sinclair, defends individual constitutional freedoms.

As you read, consider the following, questions:

1. How does the ACLU/SC characterize the students who would be affected by the DREAM Act?
2. What would be the fiscal impact of the DREAM Act, according to the viewpoint?
3. The ACLU/SC says that undocumented immigrants who have stayed in school have overcome what odds?

American Civil Liberties Union of Southern California, "Educational Access for Immigrant Students," *Take Action, American Civil Liberties Union of Southern California*, February 20, 2004. Copyright © 2004 by the American Civil Liberties Union of Southern California. Reproduced by permission.

Every year, 50,000–65,000 immigrant students who grew up in this country, attended school here, and graduated from high school here are blocked from pursuing their dreams of college education. Current laws lock undocumented students out by barring them from financial aid programs and requiring that they pay "out of state" rates. The DREAM Act, S. 1545, and Student Adjustment Act, H.R. 1684, create an alternative: putting qualified young people on track to legal status and changing the financial aid laws that currently exclude them.[1] California has taken a step toward making the college dreams of immigrant students more possible, but federal law still needs to change.

Students Who Epitomize the American Dream

Every year, tens of thousands of America's brightest high school graduates are prevented from pursuing dreams of a college education and a better future. These students, many of whom are valedictorians, honor students, class presidents or student leaders, have had to overcome numerous barriers in order to succeed. Many were brought to this country as young children and have lived here almost their entire lives, but because they don't have immigration papers, they face limited prospects for completing their education and working legally in the United States.

These talented young men and women represent some of the best that America has to offer. Our nation cannot afford to squander its most precious human resources. That is why [we] support the Student Adjustment Act (H.R. 1684) and the DREAM Act (S. 1545). This bi-partisan legislation would permit undocumented students who graduate from high school to apply for legal residency and allow these students to pay in-state tuition at public colleges and universities in their home state.

[We] urge you to support student adjustment legislation. Passage of such legislation is good for families and rewards the hard work of students who have succeeded despite tough odds. These students epitomize the American dream—let's bring them into the fold!

1. As this volume went to press, the DREAM Act was still being considered in the Senate, and the Student Adjustment Act was still in the House.

The Children of Undocumented Immigrants Deserve a College Education

The DREAM Act is a bipartisan bill pending in Congress to clear up the immigration status issues and address federal barriers to education and work confronted by the U.S.-raised children of undocumented immigrants.

Under current law, 50–65,000 students graduate from American high schools each year who have been in the U.S. more than five years but who face limited prospects for completing their education or working legally in the United States because they were originally brought here by parents lacking immigration status. Among those prevented from completing their education are valedictorians, honors students, award winners, class presidents, and student leaders.

These young people deserve a fresh start, both in fairness to them and in our national interest. The DREAM Act would address this issue in two ways:

- by deleting a federal provision that interferes with a state's right to determine which students qualify as "residents" for purposes of in-state tuition or other state education benefits; and
- by providing a mechanism for certain long-term resident immigrant students with good moral character to apply for legal residency so that they can work and otherwise fully participate in their communities.

The DREAM Act Is Economical and Fair

Positive fiscal impact: The DREAM Act would dramatically reduce dropout rates, with resulting substantial savings in criminal justice costs and use of public benefits, and it would sharply increase the amount of taxes paid by those who qualify. These fiscal contributions will pay back the educational investment within 3–4 years by conservative estimates, and thereafter taxpayers will continue to profit from the DREAM Act for decades to come.

Fairness: The DREAM Act is a recognition of the fact that the young people at issue did not have a say in the decision to come to the U.S., and it is wrong to hold them fully liable for an immigration status that was derived from their parents. They should not be legally precluded from the achievements that they are able to earn by their own talent and hard work in the land where they were raised. The DREAM Act would give them the same opportunity to excel as their classmates . . . no more and no less.

Facilitating College Access

Legislation [allowing illegal immigrants to receive college tuition discounts] would enable more states to facilitate college access among immigrant students by providing them the flexibility to offer in-state tuition to longtime resident students, regardless of their immigrant status. In addition, both proposals would provide a path to earn permanent legal residency for immigrant students who have grown up in the U.S. and demonstrated both academic excellence in our nation's schools and good moral character.

Raul Yzaguirre, December 18, 2002. www.nclr.org.

A resource: A disproportionate number of DREAM Act young people have excelled in our schools, and they are poised to repay our investment in their elementary and secondary education. They are a willing and ready American-educated workforce, many of whom want desperately to give back to their communities. Alan Greenspan and other economists and demographers tell us that we face a long-term labor crunch that threatens our economy in the decades to come, including shortages in teaching, nursing, the service sector and other occupations. DREAM Act beneficiaries can be part of the solution.

Reward character: The most compelling reason to pass the DREAM Act is the young people themselves. They are survivors, almost all of whom have overcome the odds of growing up in tough neighborhoods and impoverished immigrant families to remain in school and to succeed. Nothing could be more American. These young people deserve to be rewarded for doing the right thing, not punished.

These basic facts were provided by the National Immigration Law Center. To learn more about the DREAM Act, visit their Immigration Law and Policy page at http://www.nilc.org/immlawpolicy/index.htm.

Mario is a studious sophomore at a high school in South

Los Angeles. His mother is a garment worker, and his father is disabled. The only way he would be able to attend college is through financial aid or scholarships. [In 2003] Mario was invited into a special outreach program established by UC Berkeley for a handful of the top California students in underrepresented schools. The program promises admission and a $28,000 scholarship upon completion, but Mario won't be eligible for the crucial scholarship. Federal laws governing financial aid exclude students, like Mario, who are undocumented, even if they have grown up in this country and attended school here.

When he found out, he says, he felt that the law treated him "like a nobody, like a stranger," because of his immigration status, despite his hard work, his good grades and the fact that California is his home.

As a result, Mario has joined a youth-led campaign that the ACLU [American Civil Liberties Union] and other groups are supporting. The goal of the campaign is to engage youth in active support of the DREAM Act, which would make students like Mario eligible for financial aid and legalization. This effort follows up at the federal level on a successful state campaign the ACLU supported last year to change the tuition for students like Mario to the in-state, rather than out-of-state rate. CHIRLA-Wise-Up!, a youth political group, is leading the effort, and the group has developed trainings, an outreach plan, and a media plan to educate the community and other youth about the legislation.

"It's important for students to unite in support of this effort," said Mario. "So many of our classmates and friends are in my situation."

"Education is not a 'human right,' as some of the proponents of this goofy attitude about tuition subsidies for illegals suggest."

Subsidizing College Tuition for Illegal Immigrants Is Unfair

Ward Connerly

In the following viewpoint Ward Connerly claims that it is wrong for illegal immigrants to receive in-state tuition discounts that out-of-state and legal foreign students do not get. While he believes that illegal immigrants should be allowed to attend college, he protests the University of California's policy to give them tuition breaks. Ward Connerly is chairman of the American Civil Rights Institute and a member of the University of California Board of Regents.

As you read, consider the following questions:
1. According to Connerly, what are the requirements an illegal immigrant must satisfy to receive in-state rates?
2. How might legal foreign students who pay out-of-state tuition react to the University of California's new policy, in the author's view?
3. What subsidies for illegal immigrants are appropriate, in Connerly's opinion?

Ward Connerly, "California Is Rewriting the Constitution; Why It Must Say No to Subsidized Education for Illegal Immigrants," *The Washington Times*, February 19, 2002. Copyright © 2002 by News World Communications, Inc. Reproduced by permission.

My sense of fairness was shaped by my Uncle James, the man who raised me after my grandmother and I moved to California in the late 1940s. Uncle James made most of his important decisions in life based on what a college professor of mine, Robert Thompson, called his "knower." A "knower" is that part of your psyche that just knows what is right and what is wrong. All of us have one, but sometimes we choose to ignore what it is telling us.

And it seems to me that California Gov. Gray Davis, members of the California legislature, and the regents of the University of California (UC) system, are ignoring their knowers over the issue of college tuition breaks for illegal aliens.

Here's what's happened: Guided by a desire to give "equitable treatment" to the sons and daughters of illegal immigrants, on the rationale that children should not be held responsible for the conduct of their parents, the regents voted 17-5 (with yours truly being in the minority of that vote) to charge illegal immigrants less to attend California public universities than U.S. citizens who live in, say, Phoenix or Denver. The requirements to qualify for this subsidy are that the student must have attended a California high school for three years, graduated from high school, and file an affidavit declaring intent to seek American citizenship.

That's right. Every citizen living legally in the other 49 states will be charged a higher tuition rate in California than illegal immigrants who happen to be in California. My knower knows this is just flat wrong.

As a regent of the UC system, I know that the citizens of my state, as well as federal taxpayers, subsidize each graduate and undergraduate student's tuition to the tune of thousands of dollars each year. That is a price California citizens, largely, must pay in state taxes to ensure a top-notch university system—one that is envied throughout the country. California residents pay $3,859 in yearly tuition to attend UC, while out-of-state students pay nearly $15,000 for the same education.

I am not unsympathetic to the millions of individuals throughout the world who want to come to California to earn a decent living and pursue opportunity and freedom.

But, our federal laws are crystal clear about illegal immigration. These laws should not be cavalierly ignored or even given a big wink. It is wrong to confer a benefit on illegal residents that we do not confer on our own citizens. This is a shameful devaluation of the privilege of American citizenship, to say nothing of the inducement to greater illegal entry into the United States.

Potential Costs of Providing In-State Tuition to Illegal Immigrants

California	$133,486,714	—	$173,532,729
Texas	$48,146,250	—	$62,590,125
Florida	$22,480,307	—	$29,224,399
New York	$17,331,557	—	$22,531,024
Arizona	$14,484,000	—	$18,829,200
Illinois	$14,046,171	—	$18,260,023
North Carolina	$13,032,443	—	$16,942,176
Georgia	$10,186,714	—	$13,242,729
Washington	$7,922,000	—	$10,298,600
Colorado	$6,991,200	—	$9,088,560
New Jersey	$6,178,529	—	$8,032,087
Nevada	$5,616,321	—	$7,301,218
Virginia	$5,574,507	—	$7,246,859
Massachusetts	$4,601,679	—	$5,982,182
Oregon	$4,250,571	—	$5,525,743

Federation for American Immigration Reform, 2003. www.fairus.org.

How can we ask the working families of California—many of whom have taken out sizable loans to finance their children's college education and many of whom will never be able to afford to send their children to college—to subsidize the education of those who should not be in our country at all?

Not to be overlooked is the fact that hundreds of thousands of Californians are unemployed, due in large part to the attack against our nation by individuals who were in our country as a result of lax immigration policies and controls. Haven't we learned anything at all from the [September 11, 2001, terrorist attacks] and subsequent thereto?

Furthermore, why would any legal foreign student pay out-of-state tuition at a UC campus when by becoming illegal he or she can get a huge annual tuition cut of about $11,000?

Few are suggesting that the children of illegal residents shouldn't be allowed to attend college in California, provided that they are not a threat to national security. However, they should play by the same rules as American citizens who live in other states and simply pay out-of-state tuition. This is not much to ask.

Our state has spent billions of dollars—that's right, billions—providing illegal residents with emergency and preventative health care and other public benefits through an enormous network of hospitals and medical clinics and other taxpayer-financed expenditures. These subsidies are appropriate because our nation has a commitment to provide relief to any man, woman or child whose life and health is endangered. These are the Judeo-Christian tenets on which our culture is founded.

But, college tuition subsidies are different from health care, primarily because no one needs a college degree to sustain health and welfare. And education is not a "human right," as some of the proponents of this goofy attitude about tuition subsidies for illegals suggest.

At the end of the day, the implementation of this policy means the state of California gets to write its own, unique immigration laws. Funny—I don't recall the U.S. Constitution providing such an exemption.

Periodical Bibliography

The following articles have been selected to supplement the diverse views presented in this chapter.

American Immigration Lawyers Association | "Student Adjustment for Deserving Children," May 26, 2004. www.aila.org.

Paul Burka | "Law's New Icon: Cheryl Hopwood," Center for Individual Rights, November 11, 2003. www.cir-usa.org.

Theodore J. Davis Jr. | "Just Between Us Blacks: Closing the Educational Achievement Gap in Delaware." www.udel.edu.

The Education Trust | "Closing the Gap: Done in a Decade," *Thinking K–16*, Spring 2001.

Melissa Ezarik | "Invisible Immigrants," *District Administration*, October 2001.

Federation for American Immigration Reform | "Taxpayers Should Not Subsidize College for Illegal Aliens," May 2003. www.fairus.org.

Marla Jo Fisher | "Recalled California Governor Vetoes Bill Giving Illegal-Immigrant Students Free Ride," *Community College Week*, November 10, 2003.

S. Anne Hancock | "There's No Doubt No Child Law Works," *Atlanta Journal-Constitution*, August 4, 2004.

Roger Kimball | "Affirmative Reaction?" *City Journal*, Summer 2000.

George Manthey | "'Bell Curve' Excuse Can Lead to Lower Expectations," *Leadership*, September/October 2003.

Rod Paige | Speech given to the National Press Club, Washington, DC, September 9, 2002. www.ed.gov.

Michael Sadowski | "Closing the Gap One School at a Time," *Harvard Education Letter*, 2001.

Dan Stein | "Why Illegal Immigrants Should Not Receive In-State Tuition Subsidies," *University Business*, April 1, 2002.

United Press International | "Education Bill Won't Close Achievement Gap," December 20, 2001.

CHAPTER 2

Are Schools Justified in Restricting Students' Expression?

Chapter Preface

In 2002 students at Boyd County High School in Kentucky created a Gay-Straight Alliance (GSA) support group for those who are gay or sympathetic to gays. Believing that by allowing the club to meet, the public school was condoning homosexuality, half of the school's population and over one thousand members of the small community protested. Two years earlier the same issue had arisen at a high school in Orange, California. At the time, school board member Bill Lewis stated, "When a school authorizes a student group called the Gay-Straight Alliance, it isn't just giving kids a place to talk about how they feel. It's also giving homosexual behavior an implied stamp of approval from a tax-supported government institution. . . . And I believe that's wrong."

The American Civil Liberties Union (ACLU) filed a lawsuit charging that the Boyd County school officials violated the federal Equal Access Act by barring the GSA but allowing other clubs to meet. The law mandates that schools must let all noncurricular clubs convene or none at all. In response to the charge, the school board stopped all clubs from meeting. James Esseks, who represents the ACLU in the matter, expressed his dismay at the school's decision: "The level of reaction or resistance [the GSA is] encountering illustrates the need for a safe place for these kids to meet. Can you imagine being a gay or lesbian student in a community where people feel so free in expressing their intolerance?"

The conflict over whether or not gay and lesbian groups should be allowed to operate on high school campuses illustrates how difficult it is to decide what types of expression, if any, to restrict in schools. It could be argued that if speech supporting homosexuality is allowed, then speech advocating heterosexuality must also be permitted. Such a premise has been at the center of numerous court cases. For instance, a Christian student who was not allowed to express her beliefs during her high school's Diversity Week won a lawsuit against her school district. Diversity Week panels had been scheduled to promote acceptance of homosexuality, but views against it were excluded. Detroit federal judge Gerald Rosen called this practice "unsettling" and wrote, "All of this, of course, raises the question, among others presented here, of what 'diversity' means and whether a school may promote one view of 'diversity' over another." Although it may have upset some students to hear messages that homosexuality is sinful, those views should have been allowed, he argued.

Others respond that speech advocating heterosexuality is essentially homophobic, and thus harmful. At the heart of that debate is the question of whether homophobic, racist, or sexist speech should be allowed in schools even though it is hurtful. As a staff writer for the *Atlanta Journal-Constitution* says, "It's a long-standing and cherished principle in the American system that private persons can be pretty much as offensive as they want, as long as they aren't obscene or directly harmful to anyone else. All of us put up with many [insulting] things . . . because our disagreement or disgust does not override the freedom of others to do them." Furthermore, free speech supporters point out that suppressing students' expression, whether religious, political, or sexual, does not permit them to deal with issues openly and can lead to further prejudice.

On the other hand, many administrators suggest that allowing offensive speech in schools creates an uneasy atmosphere and disrupts education. They maintain that while the Bill of Rights guarantees everyone the right to free expression, schools are charged with the special task of protecting youth. An editorial in the *Seattle Times* contends, "A free society is for adults, who are presumed to have a certain thickness of skin. Though the Constitution 'does not end at the schoolyard gate,' as the Supreme Court once famously said, it is not available full-strength, either. . . . Any school, public or private, requires a code of conduct stricter than what the police would allow on the street."

Administrators often choose to censor all speech that may disrupt the school. This chapter explores cases in which freedom of expression comes under fire in educational settings, illustrating the challenge school officials face in allowing open discourse while maintaining a positive learning environment.

"Rights are for everyone, not just those who happen to be religious."

Allowing Religious Expression in School Violates Students' Rights

Ellen Johnson

In the following viewpoint Ellen Johnson, president of American Atheists, Inc., argues that public schools do not respect students who are not religious or who belong to a minority religion. Students have the right to be free from religious intrusion, Johnson says, yet schools incorporate religious themes, activities, and content into what should be secular education. Non-Christian students, the author claims, are often harassed. Their rights are not safeguarded by federal guidelines, which protect religious students, and their educational rights are ignored, she maintains.

As you read, consider the following questions:
1. What does the author say federal guidelines are "less than robust" in emphasizing?
2. In the author's view, how do religious groups attempt to smuggle their message into schools?
3. What is Johnson's objection to the spontaneous prayer at Texas high school football games?

Ellen Johnson, "Introduction," *Atheists' Rights and Religious Expression in the Public Schools*. Columbus, OH: American Atheists, 2000. Copyright © 2000 by American Atheists, Inc. Reproduced by permission.

Religious practices in the public schools have necessitated constant litigation and protest. In the nineteenth century, for instance, Protestants and Roman Catholics actually rioted in Baltimore, Philadelphia, and other locales over the issue of which version of the Bible—the King James Version or the Vatican's Rheims-Douay Version—would be used in the public schools. Sectarian groups protested when mandatory prayer, Bible-verse recitation, and other coercive religious practices were challenged in courts. Freethinkers, civil libertarians, even religious people who stood up against such policies have endured harassment, marginalization, and the travails associated with taking a stand in the courts simply to defend their freedom *from* religion.

The Rights of the Religious Minority

American Atheists [Inc.] is concerned that too much latitude is given to religious students and not enough respect is given to the rights of Atheists. The large amount of mail sent to American Atheists expressing anger with this situation indicates that unless changes are made, the possibility exists for confrontation in the schools over these problems.

So, while guidelines, reports, and a corpus of legal opinion often emphasize the rights of those who are religious, constantly fostering the sensibility that the public schools should be a place "not hostile to faith," those who are *not* religious encounter a lack of the same emphasis placed on *their right*, which should include governmental assurances of an educational environment free from divisive and unwanted religious intrusion.

The religiously lopsided bias of the previously published guidelines [for religious expression in public schools] has prompted American Atheists to produce the present guide to *Atheists' Rights and Religious Expression in the Public Schools.* This is a guide for those who are not religious or are of a minority religion, who encounter problems with religion in public schools whether from administrators, teachers, other students, parents, various ministries, or sectarian groups who seek to exploit these schools as a forum for religious proselytizing. It outlines *our* rights in respect to freedom *from* religion. It relies, in large part, on the same court rulings as the federal guidelines and policy statements regarding the First Amendment issued by religious and civic groups; but it seeks to tell the other side of the story on the contentious issue of religion and our schools.

There is a pressing need for this guide, for several reasons.

Guidelines Do Not Address Religious Abuse

While federal and other guidelines may be technically correct, we have found that religious groups often interpret their tone and content selectively, seeing a "green light" for numerous practices, some of which are constitutionally suspect. The so-called "guidelines" are not used for guidance, but instead are exploited for loop-holes. What is not addressed in any of the existing guidelines are the abuses of rights by Christian students, school administrators, and outside Christian organizations. As president of America's oldest Atheist organization, I receive a steady flow of letters, e-mails and phone calls from parents and students describing situations in their public schools which, if accurate, clearly violate the principle of separation of church and state. Indeed, guidelines—whether from the government or community-policy groups—appear less than robust in emphasizing what religious practices are *not* permitted, and what rights *nonreligious students* and parents have. One tough question which needs to be raised is whether the federal guidelines are crafted in sufficiently clear and strong language so as to prevent cases of religious abuse. Existing guidelines do not address the problem of abuse, either in prevention or in rectification.

Another reason for this guide is that harassment of Atheist and other nonreligious students is very much "the untold story" in the national discussion over the role of the First Amendment in public schools. In August, 1998—three years after the flurry of guidelines from the Department of Education first began—I testified as President of American Atheists before the US Civil Rights Commission looking into religious expression in schools. I noted that after more than three decades of legislation and court rulings, the issue of religion in public education "remains a controversial and contentious subject," and that no one was addressing the issue of unconstitutional religious expression in public schools. I also told the commission that even though there are 350,000 churches, mosques, temples, chapels, and other "houses of worship" in the United States, giving religious believers ample opportunity to practice their faiths, our public schools remained battlegrounds over the separation of church and state. Too much was (and is) being done to magnify the issue of religion in our schools and to find some way of injecting religious themes, activities, organizations, and content into what should, ideally, be secular institutions which have the primary goal of educating students and preparing them for societal integration and the workforce. *No one should be allowed in the public schools without an educational reason.*

Self-Policing Has Failed

I also pointed out that with all of the soothing language about "finding common ground" and the wide latitude religious groups and individuals seem to have within our public schools, there are no mechanisms to prevent and penalize unconstitutional practices and religiously motivated harassment. Simply put, throughout our nation, "self-policing" has failed. Religious groups may even be using the federal guidelines as a sort of instruction manual in hopes of finding creative, new, and legally suspect ways of continuing to interject their doctrines into the schools. In extreme cases, such as DeKalb County, Alabama, there have been so many open acts of defiance by religious groups and some school authorities that a federal judge had to implement a "monitoring" program to make sure that constitutional guidelines on the separation of church and state were being followed.

This raises another problem with the current arrangement which seems to place considerable emphasis on religious practices in public schools. Sectarian groups, many of them on the religious right, view the public education system as a doctrinal battle ground, an opportunity for extending their proselytizing outreaches. Despite those 350,000 churches and other houses of worship, and the fact that religious youngsters and parents may pray in the privacy of their own homes or on other occasions, public events—such as the annual "See You At The Pole" activity—have been organized. Some religious groups attempt to smuggle their message into the schools using ruses like character-development programs, presentations against drug and alcohol abuse, and even entertainment in the form of athletic feats or magic shows laced liberally with a fundamentalist slant.

Peters. © 1994 by the *Dayton Daily News*. Reproduced by permission.

There are constant efforts to organize Bible clubs, prayer circles, and other religion-based groups. Disputes about religious materials, even book covers bearing the Ten Commandments, often crop up. At every turn, there is a bevy of legal groups such as the American Center for Law and Justice (founded by televangelist Pat Robertson) with the staff and resources to take on legal cases as they arise.

No Penalties for Persecution

One consequence of this—and something which surprised the US Commission on Civil Rights—is that while everyone is going to considerable lengths to guarantee the rights of religious students, parents, and organizations, students who don't accept a religious message are often marginalized, harassed, and have their rights violated. I see this in the steady stream of e-mails and phone calls to American Atheists. Students who have no religious beliefs, or have serious doubts about religion, are often pressured to participate in faith-based groups and events. Some who contact us feel overwhelmed by the overt displays of religiosity in what should be a secular, educational setting—religious posters, announcements, group prayers, prayers over school intercoms, devotional activities in choruses, assemblies, Bible handouts, and much more. Buried in the federal guidelines are reminders that some of these activities are wrong, that religious groups may not foist themselves on others; but there are no concrete recommendations on how a harassment victim might respond.

Take one case involving an Atheist student from Collins, New York, who was the target of religious abuse. She had joined a chorus in her public school but refused to participate in songs of praise to a Christian "savior," on the basis that it violated her freedom of conscience. As I told the Civil Rights Commission:

> This has resulted in threats of physical violence (including the religious suggestion of "burning in hell"), and being told that she was "lying" about her nonbelief, and that we are a "Christian nation, so deal with it." There was no recourse to the student because the choral director, teachers, principal, and school board all sided against the Atheist student. . . .

I also told the Commission:

> Increasingly, American Atheists has received reports of exuberant student "prayer warriors" aggressively "sharing the good news" of their religious faith with other students who disagree or are repulsed by such proselytizing. "Prayer warriors" cannot be permitted to conduct in-your-face harassment in school hallways, lunchrooms, or lobbies. . . .

The Threat of Religion in Schools

One factor contributing to this growing problem is that many religious activities which are defended as "student-led" or "student-initiated" are, in fact, the results of organized efforts by adult, off-campus groups. We recently saw the problem in Texas where, following the June, 2000 US Supreme Court decision in *Santa Fe Independent School District v. Doe* that banned "student-initiated" prayer at high school athletic events, prayer supporters decided to disrupt football games with "spontaneous prayer." There was little genuine spontaneity about this bullying, and often it was off-campus ministers, religious groups, or churches that were organizing these "student-led" events.

While the government (and schools) are constrained by the First Amendment to be strictly neutral in respect to religion, religious groups are often far from neutral regarding their view of public schools. In preparation for the annual "See You At The Pole" event, the Southern Baptist Convention dispatched letters to 45,000 pastors across the country exhorting them to take "prayer back to our high school campuses." Local churches were urged to "join us in seeing the campus as a mission field and seizing the day to penetrate this mission field with the Gospel of Christ."

It needs to be said that despite the "guidelines," court rulings, and endless conferences over the role of religion in the public schools, we may actually look forward to *more* rather than *fewer* problems related to this issue. Religious groups can be expected to continue efforts to alter the constitution through legislation like the Religious Freedom Amendment,[1] which would allow a much wider range of sectarian worship and rituals in our schools. Even without that threat, there are serious problems with proposals which seek to use religious texts and themes in order to teach everything from history to personal values. The situation is a complex one: obviously, courses which may include references to religious ideas and history might be more appropriate in a college setting than, say, a grade school class. Even a "balanced" presentation, though, which purports to survey objectively different religious ideas and their impact on history may be fraught with problems where there are no adequate oversight mechanisms to prevent proselytizing and other abuses.

So far, the guidelines and conferences have done nothing to protect the rights of Atheist students. They have encouraged religious groups to become more aggressive in our schools; and the lack of penalties and monitoring has meant that it is religious groups and believers who appear to be the objects of considerable concern and protection. . . .

1. The amendment was defeated by the House of Representatives in June 1998.

Educational Rights of Atheists Are Ignored

Let me add a final thought here. Too often, Atheists are unjustly accused of being intolerant and dogmatic. No, we don't want to "ban religion," or persecute those who have ideas we happen to disagree with. American Atheists takes the position that even with our current dilemma over religion in the public schools, the First Amendment to the Constitution has done an excellent job of guaranteeing Americans both freedom *of* and freedom *from* religion. The principle of state-church separation has served us well in moderating the tendency of sectarian denominations to quarrel with their neighbors and impose their will on society through force. It has also been a shield for the defense of those who harbor no religious beliefs. We take the position that while the First Amendment has not always been applied consistently, as we would like it to be, it has worked well throughout the two hundred plus years of the American experience.

Rights, though, are for everyone—not just those who happen to be religious. In the debate over the role of faith in our public schools, the balance has shifted far in the direction of what are described as "religious rights." The role of students' "educational rights" has effectively been ignored.

*"Schools must not discriminate against
students who wish to engage in prayer or
religious expression."*

Allowing Religious Expression in School Protects Students' Rights

Mathew D. Staver

In the following viewpoint Mathew D. Staver asserts that students have a constitutional right to express their religious views in school. Religious activity on campus is protected by federal guidelines issued by the U.S. Department of Education in 2003, he claims. Calling these guidelines "a blessing," Staver applauds the department for withholding federal education funds from schools that discriminate against students who wish to engage in prayer or religious speech. Mathew D. Staver is president and general counsel of Liberty Counsel, a nonprofit religious civil liberties and legal defense organization.

As you read, consider the following questions:

1. In order to receive federal funds, what must public schools do to satisfy Section 9524 of the Elementary and Secondary Education Act?
2. Per the Guidelines on Constitutionally Protected Prayer, under what circumstances may teachers participate in religious baccalaureate ceremonies?
3. According to Staver, how are the new prayer guidelines unlike the guidelines issued by the Department of Education in 1996?

Mathew D. Staver, "New Federal Guidelines a Real Blessing for Public Schools," *The Liberator*, vol. 14, March 2003, pp. 1–4. Copyright © 2003 by Liberty Counsel. Reproduced by permission.

In the late afternoon of February 7 [2003], I received a call from an Associated Press (AP) reporter out of Washington, D.C., who is the top person in AP covering educational issues from grades K-12. He alerted me to new Guidelines that were to be issued that afternoon by the U.S. Department of Education regarding prayer in school. After reading the Guidelines, I was interviewed by this AP writer Friday evening, and the story was carried on the AP wire service. The next day, on Saturday, most major newspapers in America picked up the good news about the Guidelines on prayer and religious expression.

Guidelines on Prayer in Public Schools

The new "Guidelines on Constitutionally Protected Prayer in Public Elementary and Secondary Schools" come as a result of the "No Child Left Behind Act of 2001," which requires that the Secretary of Education issue guidelines on constitutionally protected prayer. These Guidelines will be a powerful weapon in the defense of religious liberty.

Section 9524 of the Elementary and Secondary Education Act ("ESEA") in 1965, as amended by the "No Child Left Behind Act of 2001," requires the Secretary to issue guidance on constitutionally protected prayer in public elementary and secondary schools. Section 9524 requires that, as a condition of receiving ESEA funds, a public school must certify in writing to its state educational agency that it has no policy which prevents or otherwise denies participation in, constitutionally protected prayer in public schools as set forth in the Guidelines.

The new Guidelines were jointly approved by the Office of the General Counsel in the Department of Education and the Office of Legal Counsel in the Department of Justice. These Guidelines reflect the current state of the law. The Guidelines can be accessed by going to Liberty Counsel's website at www.lc.org or to the Department of Education's website at www.ed.gov.

Funds Withheld from Noncompliant Schools

In order to receive federal funds under the Elementary and Secondary Education Act, a local public school must certify in writing by October 1 of each year that it is in full compliance with the Guidelines. Since the Guidelines were just issued, the initial certification this year must occur by March 15, 2003, and thereafter the certification must occur by October 1 of each year. The state educational agency must notify the United States Secretary of Education of those schools that are either not in compliance with the Guidelines or have not timely filed their certification. The General Education Provisions Act authorizes the Secretary to bring enforcement actions against recipients of federal education funds that are not in compliance with the law. This may include withholding the funds until the school complies.

The general theme of the new Guidelines, which address prayer and religious expression, essentially provides that during times and at places where students are permitted to engage in secular verbal or written expression or meetings, schools must not discriminate against students who wish to engage in prayer or religious expression. . . .

Prayer During Non-Instructional Time

During non-instructional time, schools must treat prayer and religious speech just like other secular expression. Students may

- Read their Bibles or other scriptures.
- Say grace before meals.
- Pray or study religious materials with fellow students during recess, the lunch hour, or other non-instructional time to the same extent they may engage in non-religious activities.

Students may organize prayer groups, religious clubs, and "See You At The Pole" gatherings to the same extent they are permitted to organize other non-curricular student activities. Such groups must

- Be given the same access to school facilities for assembling as is given to other non-curricular groups.
- Be allowed to advertise or announce their meetings through bulletin boards, student newspaper, or making announcements on a public address system.
- Be allowed to hand out leaflets.

Teachers are often discriminated against by school offi-

President George W. Bush on Public School Prayer

"I support voluntary, student-led prayer and am committed to the First Amendment principles of religious freedom, tolerance, and diversity. Whether Mormon, Methodist, or Muslim, students in America should be able to participate in their constitutional free exercise of religion. I believe it is wrong to forcefully expunge any mention of religion, or dilute its impact and importance, when discussing world affairs. Religion is a personal, private matter and parents, not public school officials, should decide their children's religious training. We should not have teacher-led prayers in public schools, and school officials should never favor one religion over another, or favor religion over no religion (or vice versa). I also believe that schools should not restrict students' religious liberties. The free exercise of faith is the fundamental right of every American, and that right doesn't stop at the schoolhouse door."

Ontario Consultants on Religious Tolerance, October 9, 2000. www.religioustolerance.org/ps_pra4.htm.

cials under the mistaken notion that every action of a teacher is an official representation of the school. The Guidelines state that teachers may

- Take part in religious activities where the overall context makes clear that they are not participating in their official capacities.
- Meet with other teachers during lunch or other breaks to engage in prayer or Bible studies to the same extent that they may engage in other conversation or non-religious activities.
- Participate in privately sponsored baccalaureate ceremonies.
- Meet with student religious clubs after school.
- Open their class with a minute of silence or other quiet periods during the school day to allow students to pray silently, or even not to pray, according to the students' desire.

Accommodating Religious Students

Teachers must also accommodate students, which includes:

- Allowing students to leave the school premises to en-

gage in off-site religious instruction.
- Allowing a student to opt out of objectionable curriculum.

Students may express their beliefs about religion in homework, artwork, and other written and oral assignments free from discrimination based on the religious content of their submissions.

Student Assemblies, Graduation, and Baccalaureate Ceremonies

This area of the Guidelines will prove to be a significant blessing for public school students. The Guidelines state that where "student speakers are selected on the basis of genuinely neutral, evenhanded criteria and retain primary control over the content of their expression, that expression is not attributable to the school and therefore may not be restricted because of its religious (or anti-religious) content." Thus, students may

- Engage in prayer or religious expression at student assemblies.
- Engage in prayer or religious expression during graduation. (This section of the Guidelines incorporates the legal principle arising out of our victory in the *Adler v. Duval County School Board* graduation prayer case.)

The Guidelines also say that if a school makes its facilities and related services available to other private groups, it must make the same facilities and services available on the same terms to organizers of privately sponsored, religious baccalaureate ceremonies. Teachers may participate in such service so long as they do so in their personal rather than official capacities.

These Guidelines are a blessing to public school students and teachers in grades K-12. As soon as I received the Guidelines, our office [at the Liberty Counsel] filed them in every one of our ongoing federal court cases. We are aggressively using these Guidelines to inform public school officials to maintain compliance by refraining from discriminating against students who engage in prayer or religious expression. Unlike the original Guidelines that were first issued by the Department of Education in 1996, these Guidelines have an enforcement mechanism. Any noncomplying school may lose federal education funds. These Guidelines present a significant opportunity to prevent religious discrimination in public schools. I encourage you to contact Liberty Counsel's office to obtain a copy of these Guidelines. You should then distribute these Guidelines to every teacher, administrator, school board attorney and school board member in your community.

*"Allowing students the opportunity to
publicly and genuinely voice their concerns
can act as a means of dissipating tensions."*

Suppressing Threatening Speech Infringes on Students' Rights

David L. Martinson

In the following viewpoint David L. Martinson argues that restricting students' threatening speech violates their rights and is potentially harmful. Suppressing speech drives opposition underground rather than allowing students to deal with issues in an open forum, he says. Martinson concludes that permitting such speech ultimately ensures school safety. David L. Martinson is a professor in the school of journalism and mass communication at Florida International University in North Miami.

As you read, consider the following questions:

1. The author cites a *Miami Herald* article that says the Littleton shootings convinced Dade officials that they were right in doing what?
2. What is Martinson's solution to the inevitable tension between administrators and individual constitutional rights?
3. In the author's contention, unnecessary control of student expression sends what message?

David L. Martinson, "A School Responds to Controversial Student Speech Serious Questions in Light of Columbine," *The Clearing House*, vol. 73, January 2000, p. 145. Copyright © 2000 by the Helen Dwight Reid Educational Foundation. Reproduced by permission of the Helen Dwight Reid Educational Foundation, published by Heldref Publications, 1319 18th St. NW, Washington, DC 20036-1802.

The [school shootings] of recent times suggest to some that America's public schools are beginning to more closely resemble a training ground for guerrilla warfare than institutions whose primary concern is the intellectual growth and social development of our nation's youth. The tragic loss of life in the shootings at Columbine High School in the Denver [Colorado] area in April 1999 is the most prominent among many occurrences that lead a frustrated citizenry to ask that something be done to bring a sense of normality to our schools.

Predictably, one of the first responses has been a call for increased discipline, especially in the form of control of student speech/expression. It is difficult to defend freedom of speech/expression under the best of circumstances. [Mass communication experts Melvin L.] DeFleur and [Everette E.] Dennis correctly note that

> almost all Americans will nod vigorously in agreement if asked whether they believe in freedom of the press. It ranks with motherhood, the Marines, and the American flag as a source of national esteem. However, when pressed on some specific case—such as pornography, criticism of their favorite public figure, or unfavorable stories about themselves—their assent to a free press is likely to vanish.

The problems are magnified when one moves to the public school level. It has always been difficult to defend students' rights to freedom of speech/expression—somewhat akin to defending those of the Ku Klux Klan or magazine publishers like [*Hustler*'s] Larry Flynt. In this article, however, I present arguments to support doing just that in light of an incident that took place at a Florida high school a year prior to the Columbine shootings. I believe these arguments, which have been formulated over many years, are of particular relevancy in the wake of recent events.

Administrative Overkill?

In 1998, a high school principal in Dade County (Miami) Florida called police and had nine students arrested after they published and distributed a pamphlet that they titled "First Amendment." [According to journalist Sue] Reisinger, they were "charged with hate crimes for creating an underground pamphlet containing racial slurs, sexist remarks and profanities." [She writes that,] among other things, the pamphlet included

- A picture of their principal [with] a dart board behind him, and a cartoonish dart sticking out of his forehead. . . .
- A copy of the First Amendment, with an accompanying explanatory sentence that uses the F-word. . . .
- A cartoon showing a man with facial features similar to [the principal's] engaging in a sex act while others watch.

Also in the pamphlet was an essay that declared, "I often wonder what would happen if I shot [the principal] in the head and other teachers who have p—— me off or shot the f—— bastard who thought I looked at him wrong or the airheaded cheerleader who is more concerned about what added layer of Revlon she's putting on."

Certainly not the type of material to appear in the *New York Times*—"All the News That's Fit to Print." Nevertheless, particularly when viewed in hindsight after the events in Littleton, Colorado, it is appropriate to ask, Was the principal acting prudently in having the students arrested? An editor of the *Miami Herald* suggested at the time that "the principal would make criminals out of rebellious teenagers whose worst act was to express their thoughts—sometimes ugly thoughts, but mostly provocative ones—openly." She argued that the school should not have attempted to "repress the words, or feelings behind them [but rather should have dealt with them] in an open forum of ideas, and trust that truth will win out."

A featured columnist [Carl Hiaasen] for the same newspaper charged that the school had engaged in "a textbook example of overkill." He maintained that while the pamphlet "surely isn't [the students'] best work, it is worth reading if you care about how young people are looking at the world." A reader, he asserted, would find "some of the work . . . touching in its expression of unhappiness and inner turmoil."

Fortresses of Authoritarianism

Undoubtedly, many high school administrators became livid upon reading those remarks, viewing such observations as just another example of journalists "sermonizing" from their ivory towers. Others reasonably might have suggested that if the editor and the columnist entered the "real world" in which a metropolitan area high school principal must function each day, they would quickly have become more empathetic. Interestingly, after the Columbine shootings, one of the nine young people involved in the production of the pamphlet appeared to have had second thoughts himself. It was reported [in the *Miami Herald*] that

> ... [Camilo] Palomeque says he may have been wrong after all. In the wake of the murder of 12 students and a teacher in Littleton, Colo., by two other students, Palomeque says the so-called Killian Nine acted irresponsibly when they published a vulgarity-filled pamphlet that hurled venom at student athletes and mused about "what would happen" if the school's principal were shot in the head.

As one might expect, [the article states,] "the Littleton killings . . . convinced Dade school officials that they did the right thing in [this] case." The deputy superintendent argued that "Miami-Dade schools stand out in America today for doing what we thought was right at the time. . . . No one has made a threat against the administration since then because everyone knows we take threats seriously."

Although one can understand such reactions, the fact remains that freedom of speech is a basic and intrinsic right of all Americans, including students. Further, research suggests that the public schools do a poor job teaching basic democratic values and that they too often begin to resemble fortresses of authoritarianism, institutions that perform dysfunctionally with regard to the inculcation of respect for and support of core political/philosophical/social concepts such as those that are enumerated in the Bill of Rights.

An Inevitable Tension

It is essential that school administrators understand that "there will always be tension between the interests of teachers and administrators on the one hand and individual constitutional rights on the other," [write D.M.] Gillmor, [J.A.] Barron, [T.F.] Simon, and [H.A.] Terry. . . .

I have argued in several articles that there is a solution to this tension. That solution, which takes into account the need to keep order in the school and assumes that respect and support for constitutional rights will not be fostered in an authoritarian atmosphere, rests in the school administration's adopting what is called a "preferred position" in support of freedom. More specifically, [I have written that]

> Although there will undoubtedly be times when the school administrator believes that he or she must constrain particular student expression, the scales should always be tilted in favor of openness. . . . In any instance in which restraint of student speech is contemplated, the administration should always place the burden of proof on itself—and/or on those demanding it—to show that such restraint is clearly justified and required. . . .

> That attitude is very different from the one found in too many public schools—where there is an assumption in favor of censorship, where faint-hearted school administrators continually err on the side of caution, where anything even the least bit controversial somehow becomes disruptive of "legitimate" educational concerns. . . .

Four Premises for Freedom of Expression

But, school administrators may well ask, why? Why should there be a presumption in favor of openness? Is it not being naive, at best, to speak about protecting the marketplace of ideas when one is dealing with adolescents who have no understanding of the power of the spoken or printed word? After all, look at what happened in Littleton.

An answer can be found in the work of the late Professor Thomas Emerson, for many years one of America's leading First Amendment scholars. [In *The System of Freedom of Expression*,] Emerson maintained that support for freedom of expression rests on four basic premises:

1. It is essential as a means of assuring individual self-fulfillment.
2. It is essential for advancing knowledge and discovering truth.
3. It is essential to provide for participation in decision making by all members of society.
4. It is a method of achieving a more adaptable and hence a more stable community, of maintaining the precarious balance between healthy cleavage and necessary consensus.

In the space that follows, I want to suggest how Emerson's work can have direct applicability to high school administrators and teachers—in particular, how promotion of a "preferred position" in support of freedom of expression for students is a sound policy from a variety of philosophical, social, and educational perspectives.

Ensuring Student Self-Fulfillment

Emerson argues that the "proper end of [each person] is the realization of his [or her] character and potentialities as a human being." He insists that "for the achievement of this self-realization the mind must be free [and that any] suppression of belief, opinion, or other expression is an affront to the dignity of [that person]."

Protecting "Threatening" Speech

[A] student, referred to in court documents as "George T.," served 100 days in juvenile hall during his sophomore year after showing a classmate a poem that read in part: "For I can be the next kid to bring guns to kill students at school. So parents watch your children cuz I'm back."

The court ruled the writing did not constitute a threat.

"The fact remains that 'can' does not mean 'will,'" wrote Justice Carlos R. Moreno in the court's unanimous decision. "While the protagonist . . . declares that he has the potential or capacity to kill students given his dark and hidden feelings, he does not actually threaten to do so."

Several free-speech advocates who filed briefs supporting George hailed the decision as a victory for freedom of expression.

"The court's decision makes clear that students' creative works deserve the same high level of First Amendment protection as that accorded to established poets, authors and artists," said Ann Brick, a staff attorney for the American Civil Liberties Union of Northern California.

Student Press Law Center, July 27, 2004. http://splc.org.

In relation to our public education system, this means that a primary—perhaps the ultimate—goal of the school must be the promotion of a process of self-realization in students, a process that will only occur if students are given the necessary intellectual freedom that belongs to them by the very nature of their dignity as persons.

Unnecessary control (censorship) of student expression by school authorities sends messages much stronger than anything students learn in a social studies or civics class. It teaches students that their essential worth is not measured in terms of their dignity as persons, or in the originality and vitality of their ideas, but rather in relationship to their willingness to follow orders and obey school authorities. Unfortunately, too many school authorities appear to view that message as a good thing. A school superintendent in Florida put it in stark, and frightening, terms when responding to a survey on freedom of speech in student newspapers: "The first priority of our school is to provide a safe environment. Confrontation and controversy lead to unsafe conditions. The second priority of our schools is to educate students so they can grow up and become gainfully employed."

Mark Goodman, the executive director of the Student Press Law Center, argues that "the values [students] learn [in high school] are the values they take into their lives." Emerson would no doubt argue that our schools do not serve society if the primary values students learn center around avoiding controversy and becoming gainfully employed. Surely that is not the way a democratic society wishes to judge the value of each of its citizens.

Discovering the Truth

The poet John Milton, writing in 1644, penned perhaps the most eloquent plea for free speech ever written:

> [T]hough all the winds of doctrine were let loose to play upon the earth, so Truth be in the field, we do injuriously by licensing and prohibiting to misdoubt her strength. Let her and Falsehood grapple; who ever knew truth put to the worse, in a free and open encounter?

Milton's words "had very little effect [and] were not widely disseminated at the time," [according to mass media experts E.] Emery and [M.] Emery. In fact, Milton later became a censor. His portrayal of an almost cosmic battle between truth and falsehood, however, was "picked up nearly a hundred years later by people all over the world," [write]

Emery and Emery. In America, "this passage marked the beginnings of what has become an underlying theme of First Amendment theory: the marketplace of ideas theory [which holds that] truth is best secured in the open marketplace of ideas," [according to] Gillmor et al. That is what Emerson is referring to in his second premise.

School administrators often protest, however, that particular student speech that they find objectionable is not truthful, at least not in their eyes. John Stuart Mill would retort that "there may be a particle of truth within a wrong opinion; if the wrong opinion is suppressed, that particle of truth may be lost." That is the point a tenth-grade student made in regard to the uproar resulting from the administration's response to the Dade County "First Amendment" pamphlet cited earlier. The teenager, a student at the school concerned, wrote an article for the *Miami Herald* in which he said,

> At [my school] there is a poor working relationship between students and school staff. The security staff often exhibit prison guard mentality. . . . Security personnel confront students routinely for minor violations. . . . This overreactive approach maintains focus on menial problems, allowing more severe problems to continue. Drugs and substance abuse are a major problem. Gang activity and violence are something to avoid and tolerate every day.

In other words, although there was a considerable amount of material in the pamphlet that was sexist, racist, and profane, there may have also been a certain amount of truth that needed to be faced. Instead of calling for arrests, the school administration might have used it as an educational opportunity to engage in a process whereby administrators, faculty, and students would "thoughtfully explor[e] . . . the pamphlet's content [while] discussing its conflict [in an effort to defuse] its anger," Reisinger [writes]. In doing so, the "whole" truth may well have been better served.

Participation in Decision Making

Emerson argues that "once one accepts the premise of the Declaration of Independence—that governments 'derive their just powers from the consent of the governed'—it follows that the governed must, in order to exercise their right of consent, have full freedom of expression both in forming individual judgments and in forming the common judgment."

Although students obviously do not govern the school, many activities—such as student government—are established precisely to give them some experience in the dynamics of decision making in a democratic and pluralistic society. The only way to make that participation meaningful is to provide for a genuine exchange of ideas, and that will only occur when students are allowed a reasonable degree of freedom. The U.S. Supreme Court made that clear many years ago in a case involving a student belonging to the Jehovah's Witnesses (*West Virginia State Board of Education v. Barnette*, 1943) and the right of that student not to be forced to salute the flag. [R.S. Erikson, N.R. Luttbeg, and K.L. Tedin write:]

> That they are educating the young for citizenship is reason for scrupulous protection of Constitutional freedoms of the individual, if we are not to strangle the free mind at its source and teach youth to discount important principles of our government as mere platitudes.

> By unnecessarily restricting student speech and by overreacting on those occasions when students do raise questions in a perhaps less than orthodox manner, any effort to "teach" students the importance of active citizen participation in a democratic society is "delegitimized. . . . [In fact,] the disjuncture between the democratic creed and what actually goes on in school tends to inhibit political learning."

A Balance Between Stability and Change

"Freedom of expression is [also] a method of achieving a more adaptable and hence more stable community," according to Emerson. It is a means "of maintaining the precarious balance between healthy cleavage and necessary consensus." Commenting on that fourth premise of Emerson, communication scholars [R.R.] Middleton and [B.F.] Chamberlin assert the following:

> Where there is freedom of expression, dissidents may work their ideas into the social fabric without resorting to a violent underground cell. Worthless ideas can be rejected with little threat to the stability of society. Where freedom prevails, consensus supports orderly change. Free expression therefore promotes both stability and flexibility, tradition and change.

One might suggest that the likelihood of a reoccurrence of violent incidents might be lessened if school administrators will adopt a "preferred position" in favor of maximum freedom for student expression. At a minimum, allowing students the opportunity to publicly and genuinely voice their concerns can act as a means of dissipating tensions because the very process can "act as a safety valve, allowing [students] to participate in change rather than [forcing them to] seek influence through antisocial acts," [write] Middleton and Chamberlin.

School administrators need to be reminded again and again that "suppression drives . . . opposition underground," [as] Middleton and Chamberlin [assert]. When it explodes, the damage is often far greater than would have been the case if school administrators had refrained from overreacting to a supposed threat presented by a few students wishing to ventilate their feelings, even if they do so in a less than orthodox manner.

Give Students a Voice

The tenth-grade student who wrote the article for the *Miami Herald* appeared to have a surprisingly strong grasp of what Emerson proposes when he wrote,

> The [students concerned] attempted to focus attention on some real challenges faced by students at the school. . . . [School administrators should] put the responsibility back on the students and give the "problem students" a chance to problem-solve and take responsibility. The school system often squashes those who dare to speak or challenge rules that are unfair. . . . Give the students a voice. This is the time in our lives that we learn to take on challenges.

> *"Case law illustrates that students can be disciplined for verbal, written, or symbolic expression that is obscene, intimidating, or threatening."*

Suppressing Threatening Speech Is Necessary and Constitutional

David L. Stader

The following viewpoint, written as a guide for high school administrators, presents several court cases as evidence of the legality of school threat policies. Since all threats should be treated as if they are legitimate, says author David L. Stader, codes that restrict intimidating speech are necessary to ensure student safety. The rights of students who are disciplined for such speech are not violated but in fact protected by due process, he maintains. David L. Stader is an assistant professor of educational leadership at the University of Wyoming.

As you read, consider the following questions:
1. What did the court say was the central issue in *Lovell v. Poway Unified School District?*
2. According to the First Circuit Court's ruling, under what circumstances can students be disciplined for off campus conduct?
3. What are the advantages of a flexible threat policy, as explained by the author?

David L. Stader, "Responding to Student Threats: Legal and Procedural Guidelines for High School Principals," *The Clearing House*, vol. 74, March 2001, p. 221. Copyright © 2001 by the Helen Dwight Reid Educational Foundation. Reproduced by permission of the Helen Dwight Reid Educational Foundation, published by Heldref Publications, 1319 18th St. NW, Washington, DC 20036-1802.

The safe schools issue is a politically charged quagmire that arouses strong emotions. Addressing student rights within that milieu is one of the more difficult challenges facing school principals. Balancing student rights with emotion becomes especially difficult when principals are faced with student threats. To make matters more difficult, legal challenges to administrative responses to student threats are always a possibility. Such challenges typically cite First Amendment (freedom of expression) and/or Fourteenth Amendment (due process) violations. Therefore, in this article I will focus on some of the legal and procedural guidelines pertaining to freedom of expression and due process in how teachers and administrators handle student verbal or symbolic threats.

Freedom of Expression at School

Student rights to expression on school grounds were initially outlined in *Tinker v. Des Moines School District* (1969). This is the famous "black armband" case in which several students, including John and Mary Beth Tinker, planned to wear black armbands to school to protest U.S. involvement in the Vietnam War. After hearing of the plans, principals in the district met and adopted a policy that prohibited the wearing of armbands to school. John Tinker wore his armband the next day, refused to remove it, and was suspended from school.

In a well-written opinion, Justice Fortas established the concept that "it can hardly be argued that either students or teachers shed their constitutional rights to freedom of speech or expression at the schoolhouse gate. . . . The constitution says that Congress (and the States) may not abridge the right to free speech. This provision means what it says. . . ." Student expression can be suppressed if it causes disruption in the school. However, suppression should not occur because the expression makes teachers or administrators uncomfortable or because of some vague fear of disruption.

Indecent or Threatening Speech Can Be Censored

Courts have never granted the same rights of expression to students on school grounds that ordinary citizens possess in everyday life. Restrictions on student expression were clarified in *Bethel School District No. 403 v. Fraser* (1986). Fraser, in spite of warnings from two of his teachers, delivered a sexually explicit nominating speech at an assembly for a fellow student running for elective school office. During his speech, Fraser repeatedly referred to his candidate "in terms of an elaborate, graphic, and explicit sexual metaphor," and as a result was suspended from school for three days. Fraser sought judicial relief, citing a violation of his First Amendment rights. On appeal, the U.S. Supreme Court ruled in favor of the school district. In its ruling, the Court established that schools can discipline students for indecent speech and that "nothing in the constitution prohibits (schools) from insisting that certain modes of expression are inappropriate and subject to sanctions."

In another First Amendment case involving student speech, the U.S. Ninth Circuit Court of Appeals again ruled in favor of the district in *Lovell v. Poway Unified School District* (1996). At the end of a long day, student Lovell (then fifteen years old) approached the school counselor in an effort to change her schedule. The counselor informed Lovell that the classes she had finally arranged were overloaded, and the counselor refused to change Lovell's schedule. At that point Lovell either said, "I'm so angry, I could just shoot someone" (Lovell's version), or, "If you don't give me this schedule change, I'm going to shoot you" (the counselor's version). Both parties agreed that Lovell immediately apologized, and the counselor made the schedule changes.

Two days later, after a conference with Lovell, her parents, and the counselor, an assistant principal suspended Lovell for three days. Lovell's parents accepted the suspension but later objected to the wording on the referral form and asked that the form be removed from her record. The school did not respond and Lovell's parents alleged a First Amendment violation. The court ruled that threats of violence are not protected speech, reasoning that the central issue was not whether the student actually meant what he or she said, but rather, "[t]he result turns upon whether a reasonable person in these circumstances should have foreseen that his or her words would . . . [appear threatening].". . .

Written Expression

In a case of written expression that was not part of the curriculum, a seventh grade student was suspended for three days for drawing a confederate flag in his notebook, in violation of school policy (*West v. Darby Unified School District No. 260* [2000]). In response to several racial incidents in the past, the district had adopted a policy forbidding racially intimidating symbols or speech. Student West drew the flag on a piece of paper in math class and was reported by a fellow student to his teacher. The student's father filed suit against the district, alleging, among other things, a violation of his son's First Amendment rights and the district's failure to demonstrate that the student's drawing created disruption before it applied sanctions. The court ruled that the district could suppress such expression and that a First Amendment claim was not valid. Further, based on past experience and a defensible policy, the district did not have to demonstrate disruption before suppressing such speech.

Expression Off School Property

Suppression of student speech off campus in non-school sponsored activities can be more problematic. However, in *Fenton v. Stear* (1976) the Western District Court of Pennsylvania upheld the suspension of a student for shouting a derogatory comment at a teacher in a shopping mall parking lot. In a similar case, the First Circuit Court ruled that students could be disciplined for off-premises conduct when the conduct causes disruption at school. In *Donovan v. Richie* (1995), a student developed a list of fellow students that was derogatory in nature. The list was brought to school, duplicated, and found by a faculty member. The First Circuit upheld a ten-day suspension from school. These cases indicate that students can be disciplined for verbal or written expression off campus if the expression causes disruption in the school or interferes with a teacher's ability to maintain discipline.

The Internet creates more problems for principals. In *Beussink v. Woodland R-IV School District* (1998), the Eastern District Court of Missouri was presented with just such an issue. Student Beussink created a Web site at home that was critical of the school, the principal, and some of the teachers. The site remained secret until Beussink's angry girl-friend showed the site to her computer teacher. The principal initially suspended Beussink for five days and on later reflection suspended him for an additional five. The district had an attendance policy that penalized the grades of absent students. When the district applied that policy to Beussink, he went to the courts for relief. The court ruled that since the Web site did not cause substantial disruption in the school, the additional grade penalty could not be applied.

Student Threats Are No Joking Matter

While the vast majority of student threats prove to be idle, in virtually all jurisdictions even threatening to harm another person is a crime. Beyond the law, however, common sense dictates that all student threats must be taken seriously and investigated so as to protect the safety of others in the school environment. Suspending a threatening student provides school and law enforcement authorities the time to conduct a thorough assessment of the threat and to make an informed decision regarding the needs of the school and community, as well as those of the threatening student. . . .

It is often not easy to determine whether a student is joking or serious when making a threat. School officials who attempt to make that distinction do so at their own risk, as well as the risk of others. . . . Even where it appears likely that a student's threat has been made in jest, at least a brief suspension from school is warranted in order to teach that violence is no joking matter.

Charles Patrick Ewing, *Insights*, January/February 2000.

To further illustrate, the Commonwealth Court of Pennsylvania upheld the expulsion of an eighth grade student who created a Web site titled "Teacher Sux" (*J.S. v. Bethlehem Area School District* [2000]). The Web site, developed at the student's home, consisted of several pages that made derogatory comments about the student's math teacher and the principal. The site solicited contributions for a "hit man" and included a picture of the math teacher with a severed head dripping with blood and her picture morphing into Adolph Hitler's. Consequently, the math teacher was unable to continue in her position and requested a leave of absence for emotional stress. After some delay, expulsion proceedings were begun against the student. As part of their ruling, the justices stated that

> in this day and age where school violence is becoming more commonplace school officials are justified in taking . . . seriously threats against faculty and other students. Given the contents of Student's web-site and the effect it had upon [math teacher], . . . the School District did not violate Student's rights under the First Amendment.

Procedural Due Process

Students facing suspension from public schools have property and liberty interest that qualifies them for due process protection. Consequently, school policies and due process procedures are important considerations. There are two forms of due process: procedural and substantive. Legal appeals of student suspension or expulsion often cite school district violations of both procedural and substantive due process.

Procedural due process involves the steps taken in decision making. For school principals those steps were established by the Supreme Court in *Goss v. Lopez* (1975). Students facing short-term suspensions, defined as ten days or fewer, must be given written or oral notice of the charges against them and, if the student denies the charge, an explanation of the evidence available and a chance to refute the charges. Procedural due process should be completed before the student is removed from school.

However, if the continued presence of the student endangers others, the necessary notices and hearing can follow as soon as practicable. *C.B. and T.P. v. Driscoll* (2000) is an example. T.P. was involved in a fight, refused to calm down, continued to shout obscenities, disobeyed school administrators, and injured the principal. T.P. was taken to the police station, where her mother retrieved her. The student and her mother discussed the incident later that day by telephone with the principal, and T.P. was suspended for fighting, using obscenities, and refusing to cooperate. As part of her suit against the principal, T.P. alleged that the decision to suspend her was made before the telephone conversation and before she could give her side of the story.

The Eleventh Circuit Court ruled that T.P. was properly

removed from school because she posed a danger. The court defined the issue in this case to be whether T.P. had the chance to explain herself before the decision to suspend her was made. The court concluded that the telephone call satisfied the requirements of *Goss v. Lopez*. Further, "a . . . decision to suspend . . . may be made . . . as long as the disciplinarian . . . holds a prompt . . . hearing at which the preliminary decision to suspend can be reversed."

Substantive Due Process

Substantive due process involves the fairness or reasonableness of a decision. One aspect of substantive due process is notice. Students should know in advance that certain acts may result in some form of sanction. Substantive due process also requires that decisions be based on reasonable evidence, that they not include hearsay evidence or unsubstantiated rumor, and that decisions be based on some legitimate purpose. Legitimacy means there should be a relationship between the decision and some educational purpose. When that relationship is clearly present, judges are especially reluctant to overrule school officials.

The intense political pressure for safer schools has stimulated several rules of discipline, often labeled "zero-tolerance" policies. Such policies can, however, create a false sense of security, and there is no evidence that they have been effective in the long-term reduction of school violence. In fact, excessively punitive practices may contribute to student alienation and create a toxic school environment. The very policies and practices designed to prevent school violence may create more violence.

Nevertheless, when threats do occur it is essential that school officials react as if each one were legitimate. An "airport mentality" may represent the best response policy to student threats. All threats in an airport are taken seriously, and signs warning about jokes abound. However, not all threats in an airport result in long-term incarceration. In a school, an airport policy is a flexible policy that contains a wide range of options. Flexibility allows administrators to investigate, determine the seriousness of the threat, and assess the impact of the threat before choosing among a variety of sanctions. A flexible policy also allows students to be treated as individuals and helps to ensure that procedural and substantive due process requirements are met. . . .

Intimidating Expression Can Be Restricted

Students do have a constitutional right to freedom of expression that cannot be suppressed simply because the expression makes school officials uncomfortable or causes some undifferentiated fear of disruption. However, case law illustrates that students can be disciplined for verbal, written, or symbolic expression that is obscene, intimidating, or threatening.

> "*School officials may not ban student expression just because they don't like it—or because they think it might cause conflict.*"

School Dress Codes Limit Students' Freedom of Expression

Charles Haynes

According to Charles Haynes in the following viewpoint, numerous lawsuits have found that school districts have overly broad and unconstitutional dress codes. Because a wide range of student expression, including political and religious speech on clothing, is protected by the Constitution, school districts will lose most of the cases against them, he predicts. Haynes argues that creating an environment that is open to diversity can create conflict, but such controversy is essential to free societies. Charles Haynes is a senior scholar of the First Amendment Center, which works to preserve First Amendment freedoms.

As you read, consider the following questions:
1. How do school officials overreact when trying to prevent controversy, according to the author?
2. Per the *Tinker* decision, what evidence must a school have in order to legally ban student expression?
3. In the Elliot Chambers case, what did the judge say is the responsibility of the school and its community?

Charles Haynes, "T-Shirt Rebellion in the Land of the Free," *First Amendment Center*, March 14, 2004. Copyright © 2004 by *First Amendment Center*. Reproduced by permission.

If you think students are apathetic these days, you haven't been reading their T-shirts.

From the Confederate flag to gay rights, student shirts are walking billboards for every conceivable cause—blaring messages that are often provocative, sometimes funny, but always difficult to ignore.

School officials are not amused. Eager to prevent controversy or conflict, many administrators overreact by banning all messages in the name of "safety, order and discipline."

But in the land of the free, it's hard to censor without a fight. Even kids who don't know much about the First Amendment or current law know a lot about "free speech." Heavy-handed school administrators often find themselves fighting a lawsuit.

An Increasing Number of Lawsuits

The Albemarle County, Va., school district probably didn't think twice when they passed a dress code policy that, among other things, prohibits students from wearing clothing that depicts images of weapons.

But when 13-year-old Alan Newsom was recently told to turn his National Rifle Association T-shirt inside out, he refused. Alan's lawsuit is working its way through the courts,[1] but he won an important victory when a federal appeals court barred the school district from enforcing the policy while the lawsuit is pending. The court indicated that the dress code is too broad—and may be unconstitutional.

Sweeping attempts to shut down student speech frequently backfire. [In 2003] a Georgia school district decided to ban all T-shirts with the Confederate flag. Overnight the most popular T-shirt was one that says: "Jesus and the Confederate Battle Flag: Banned From Our Schools But Forever in Our Hearts."

Meanwhile in North Carolina, a principal told students that he wouldn't allow "gay, fine by me" T-shirts in his school. A New Jersey school banned a T-shirt with the word "redneck." And so it goes around the nation.

School districts may win some of these lawsuits and

1. The case was settled in a sealed agreement in February 2004.

fights—but they'll probably lose most of them. Here's why: In 1969, the U.S. Supreme Court ruled in *Tinker v. Des Moines Independent School District* that students don't "shed their constitutional rights to freedom of speech and expression at the schoolhouse gate."

The *Tinker* case involved several students who decided to wear black armbands to school to protest U.S. involvement in Vietnam. Hearing about the planned protest, school officials quickly enacted a no-armband policy. When the students were told they couldn't wear their armbands (even though other symbols were allowed), they sued.

Allowing Offensive Clothing in Schools Is the American Way

It's a long-standing and cherished principle in the American system that private persons can be pretty much as offensive as they want, as long as they aren't obscene or directly harmful to anyone else. All of us put up with many things that insult, annoy or anger us—or turn our stomachs—because our disagreement or disgust does not override the freedom of others to do them.

That ought to go for something as mundane as the T-shirts kids choose to wear at school, as long as they aren't obscene.

Atlanta Journal-Constitution, July 27, 2001.

In finding for the students, the Court made clear that school officials may not ban student expression just because they don't like it—or because they think it might cause conflict. The school must have evidence that the student expression would lead to either (a.) a substantial disruption of the school environment, or (b.) an invasion of the rights of others.

The *Tinker* standard gives strong protection to political and religious speech by students in public schools. And most courts are likely to view a wide range of student expression from "redneck" to "gay, fine by me" as protected speech—unless the school can demonstrate with reasonable evidence that the speech will cause a "substantial disruption."

Tinker isn't the last word, however. In a 1986 case (*Bethel v. Fraser*), the Supreme Court ruled that school officials could prohibit vulgar speech at a school assembly. Such speech, said the Court, is different from the purely political speech protected under *Tinker.* The Court put it this way:

> The freedom to advocate unpopular and controversial views in schools and classrooms must be balanced against society's countervailing interest in teaching students the boundaries of socially appropriate behavior.

Where does that leave school officials? The courts have given them a free hand to ban student speech that is clearly vulgar, lewd or obscene. And the courts mostly defer to administrators to regulate student speech that is "school-sponsored" (as in the school newspaper). But all other student speech is still protected under *Tinker.*

Maintaining Diversity

Consider the case of Elliot Chambers, the Minnesota student who was told that he couldn't wear a shirt with the message "Straight Pride." The school claimed that the shirt offended some students and pointed out that there had been several hostile incidents involving gay students.

But Chambers sued, saying that the ban on his shirt was unconstitutional. A federal district court agreed. Applying *Tinker*, the judge found that Chambers' shirt was not directly connected to the disruptions claimed by the school.

"While the sentiment behind the 'Straight Pride' message appears to be one of intolerance," wrote the judge, "the responsibility remains with the school and its community to maintain an environment open to diversity and to educate and support its students as they confront ideas different from their own."

Is ensuring "an environment open to diversity" sometimes messy or offensive? Of course it is. That's what freedom is all about. Most Americans wouldn't have it any other way.

| *"By having a dress code, students know there are expectations and guidelines that they must adhere to."*

School Dress Codes Are Necessary and Constitutional

Stephen Daniels

According to the following viewpoint, school dress codes promote school safety and foster a positive learning environment. Specifically, Stephen Daniels writes, dress codes reduce conflict associated with name brand and gang clothing, decrease the gap between poor and rich students, and encourage a sense of belonging that contributes to overall order and discipline. The author asserts that dress codes are constitutional, citing court cases that found they do not infringe on students' rights or suppress their speech. Daniels is director of research for the North Carolina Family Policy Council.

As you read, consider the following questions:
1. What are the benefits of school uniforms, as cited in the U.S. Department of Education's Manual on School Uniforms?
2. The author cites the Long Beach School District's uniform policy as decreasing crime by what percent?
3. What are the three Ps of school safety?

Stephen Daniels, "Student Dress Policies: The Success of School Uniforms and Dress Codes," *Findings*, May 2001. Copyright © 2001 by the North Carolina Family Policy Council. All rights reserved. Reproduced by permission of the author.

One survey of schools nationwide conducted by the National Association of Elementary School Principals (NAESP) revealed that one out of five (21 percent) public, private and parochial school principles had either instigated a uniform policy, were currently writing one, or had it on their agenda for consideration. With so many schools and school districts adopting school dress policies, it is important to understand why so many have chosen to do so.

The purpose for most, if not all, schools that are adopting uniforms and dress codes is to address the issues of discipline and academic achievement. Classroom disruptions are commonplace in today's schools and having methods in place to promote a better learning environment have never been more important. Furthermore, little debate remains over the dangers and pressures that exist in schools today. With the increased displays of school violence, many school officials, parents and students have become more determined to find solutions.

The Benefits of School Uniforms

In determining the effectiveness of school dress policies, there is no more compelling evidence that the feedback from the school principals themselves. Though the majority of public schools do not require uniforms, the feedback is very positive from those who do. According to one survey conducted by the NAESP, principals of schools that have uniform policies in place believe that students stay more disciplined and focused in their studies and feel less peer pressure.

According to the study, principals identified the following effects of school uniforms: 79 percent believed uniforms positively affected classroom discipline; 67 percent saw an improvement in student concentration; 62 percent noticed a positive effect on school safety; 72 percent saw an increase in school spirit; 85 percent noted a better perception of the school by the community; and 75 percent indicated a positive effect on peer pressure among students.

In North Carolina, the feedback from Halifax County is also positive. Dr. Viola Vaughan, principal at Southeast Halifax High School said that their school uniform policy has done a lot for the students both academically and behaviorally. "Discipline issues have decreased tremendously," she said, "when children look around at each other, they don't see the name brands and clothing that often divides them." Dr. Vaughan pointed out that even school assemblies are quieter because students act more respectfully. Alan Sledge, assistant principal at Brawley Middle School in Halifax County, said that their uniform policy was "very effective and places a very valuable role on the academic setting because the kids are more focused on their books over their clothes."

The Positive Impact of School Dress Codes

Feedback on school dress codes has also been positive. According to Don Woodard, a high school principal in Johnston County, the students' "demeanor is better and there are fewer disruptions because of teasing, or students being uncomfortable because of the apparel that others are wearing." He also pointed out that the students have more "poise and are more well-behaved when they have the sense of being dressed for the occasion of learning." Commenting on his school's dress code, Shelly Marsh, a middle school principal also from Johnston County, said: "We have high expectations. . . . Students' attitudes are different according to their dress."

Along with school principals, the U.S. Department of Education has acknowledged the positive effect that school uniforms can have. In their publication "Manual on School Uniforms," which was ordered to be sent to every school district in the United States by President Clinton, the Department of Education cited the following potential benefits of school uniforms: (1) decreasing violence and theft; (2) preventing gang members from wearing gang clothing at school; (3) instilling student discipline; (4) helping to resist peer pressure; (5) helping students concentrate on academics; and (6) aiding in the recognition of intruders.

Promoting School Safety

Of all the potential benefits of school dress policies, none is more important than improving school safety. With student violence constantly making the headlines, the clamor for solutions continues to grow. Safety in schools today is essential, and creating an environment that reduces incidents of intimidation and violence is necessary for students to learn effectively. Unfortunately, the demand for high priced designer clothing often puts students at risk of theft and violence from other students. Clothing that indicates affiliation with gangs is also a problem and can cause intimidation and fear in schools.

The Importance of School Dress Codes

To counter violence in classrooms and to improve the quality of education, dress codes are being implemented throughout our nation's public schools. Dress codes promote school safety by decreasing school violence and serve to enhance the learning environment of schools.

Many public school administrators maintain that dress codes reflect community values and create a positive educational environment. According to educators, dress codes promote student self-respect, maintain classroom discipline, discourage peer pressure to buy extravagant clothing, and make classrooms safe. Moreover, some educators have reported that dress codes have reduced the number of fights in schools and improved scholastic achievements and student attendance. Almost twenty five percent of the nation's public elementary, middle, and junior high schools are expected to implement dress codes.

An educational institution may prescribe reasonable dress codes. Recent court decisions have noted that an educational institution must demonstrate that the dress code is reasonable and rationally related to a legitimate pedagogical purpose. Public schools have enacted a wide array of dress codes. Some schools have elected to establish mandatory dress codes or school uniforms. Other districts have prohibited certain types of clothing or have adopted a voluntary dress code. In public schools where violence is a recurrent problem, dress codes proscribe gang-related clothing, such as jewelry, insignias, and certain types and colors of clothes.

The Long Beach Unified School District was the first public school district to enact a mandatory uniform policy. The Long Beach dress code policy affects nearly 60,000 elementary and middle school students. Long Beach Superintendent Carl A. Cohn documented that the enactment of a school dress code resulted in a 32% decrease in school suspensions, a 51% decrease in fighting and an 18% decrease in vandalism with a significant improvement in attendance rates.

Max J. Madrid, "Student Dress Codes: Constitutional Requirements and Policy Suggestions," 1999. www.modrall.com.

The National School Safety and Security Services, an organization that consults nationwide on school safety and crisis preparedness issues, supports school uniforms and dress codes as a way to "contribute toward improving the school climate" because it "can play a significant role in reducing security threats and improving school safety." According to this safety organization, dress codes and uniforms can help reduce potential problems by: (1) reducing conflict stemming from socioeconomic status, such as comments and personal attacks about who has better clothing; (2) reducing ways in which gang members can identify themselves which, in essence, is a form of intimidation and creates fear; (3) reducing the risk of students being robbed of expensive clothing, jewelry, etc.; (4) in the case of uniforms, helping school administrators to more easily identify nonstudents, trespassers, and other visitors in the hallways who stand out in the crowd.

Notable evidence of the effects of a student dress policy can be seen from the aftermath of California's Long Beach school district implementing mandatory school uniforms. Since they began requiring uniforms, crime in the school district has dropped by 91 percent, suspensions have decreased by 90 percent, sex offenses have been reduced by 96 percent and vandalism is down 69 percent. Interestingly, these improvements came about without any other security measures having been implemented at the time uniforms became mandatory. In addition, a study released by the Harvard School of Education found that the Long Beach school district was among six districts in the nation's 34 largest cities that dramatically reduced their dropout rates. During the past five years, dropout rates have declined from 11.2 to 2.7 percent.

The Center for the Prevention of School Violence, though not endorsing any specific dress code policies, points out that each of the "three Ps of school safety"—"place" (physical security of the school), "people" (those in the school) and "purpose" (mission of the school)—can be impacted by school dress policies. This is because dress policies define what is appropriate for the school setting while impacting the way in which people relate and interact with one another. The Center acknowledges that though the research on student dress policies is limited, the anecdotal evidence supports the existence of some form of student dress policy.

It is important to remember that the solution to school violence does not lie in one single approach—certainly not in school dress policies alone. Yet, because of the likely benefit of curbing school violence, they should be considered along with other solutions.

Self-Esteem and School Unity

Student dress policies can also benefit students far beyond keeping them safe. Schools with uniforms say that their students have better self-esteem because without the name brand clothing on display, the students are placed on an equal level. Poorer students do not feel and are not treated as inferior because they don't have nice clothes. This equality also seems to create a sense of school unity. Dr. Viola Vaughan and Allan Sledge, both principals from Halifax County, have witnessed an increase in school unity since uniforms were required.

Dr. Arnold Goldstein, head of the Center for Research on Aggression at Syracuse University, agrees. He believes that uniforms encourage a "sense of belonging" because they promote a feeling of community among the students and help make a troubled student feel like part of a supportive whole. These effects contribute to a school's overall sense of order and discipline. As a result, the learning environment improves—making it easier for teachers to teach and for students to learn. . . .

Dress Codes Do Not Infringe on Rights

Though student dress policies have seen rapid success in schools nationwide, there is some opposition to their use. School uniforms are most often criticized because some contend that they infringe upon a student's First Amendment right to freedom of expression by mandating that students wear certain types of clothing. However, recent court rulings indicate that student dress policies withstand legal challenges as long as they adhere to some basic principles.

In January 2001, school uniform policies won a huge victory when the 5th U.S. Circuit Court of Appeals rejected the plaintiff's argument that uniforms do not improve the academic environment, dampen student expression, and infringe on religious rights. The court said that the policy was "viewpoint neutral" and justified because of its "substantial government interest" in improving education. The court added that because the school board's purpose for implementing the uniform policy was to raise test scores and improve student behavior, it in no way served to suppress student speech.

A federal district court upheld a restrictive dress code in Jefferson County, Kentucky, and found that the dress code was created to "help reduce violent gang activity, ease tensions between students who fight over attire, aid school officials in identifying campus intruders, and promote student safety in general." Therefore, the court concluded that the students' interest in expressing themselves through their choice of clothes was outweighed by the school's attempt to create a "safe and peaceful environment."

Overall, most courts agree that student dress policies may be established as long as the intent for the policy is related to a legitimate government interest (i.e. to maintain discipline or encourage academics). . . .

Dress Policies Are in the School's Best Interest

The positive feedback from school officials makes a strong case for the benefits of student dress policies. There is little doubt that some form of policy, whether uniforms or dress codes, will have a positive impact on the behavior and academic performance of students. Therefore, one might conclude it is in the best interest of each school district to adopt some form of policy.

Periodical Bibliography

The following articles have been selected to supplement the diverse views presented in this chapter.

Catherine Bennett — "Schools Are Skirting the Real Dress Issues," *Guardian*, June 24, 2004.

John Bolt — "School's In: Look Out!" *Acton Commentary*, September 5, 2001.

Jingle Davis and Chandler Brown — "Politics Ends, Football Begins with Kickoffs —Hot High School Issues: Prayer, Flag Controversies Fail to Upstage Games," *Atlanta Journal-Constitution*, September 30, 2000.

Julia Duin — "Campus Ministry Mired in Civil Rights Battle," *Insight on the News*, June 26, 2000.

First Amendment Schools — "What Are the Constitutional Objections to Mandatory Dress Codes and Uniform Policies?" www.firstamendmentschools.org.

David L. Hudson Jr. — "Clothing, Dress Codes & Uniforms: Overview," First Amendment Center. www.firstamendmentcenter.org.

Jeremy Leaming — "Paige's Religious Preference: Education Secretary's Promotion of Christian Schooling Gets Bad Grades from Civil Liberties Boosters," *Church & State*, May 2003.

Eli Lehrer — "Another Result of Racial Politics on Campus: Unfree Speech," *American Enterprise*, April/May 2003.

Kathleen Modenbach — "School Uniform Rules Conceal Students' Unique Identities (NOT!)," *Education World*, 2002.

Linda Starr — "Stop Tolerating Zero Tolerance," *Education World*, 2002.

Mathew D. Staver — "Students Suspended for Passing Out Candy Canes with Religious Messages," *Liberator*, February 2003.

Robert Strauss — "A Few Wrinkles in the New Dress Code," *New York Times*, September 7, 2003.

Jennifer Swadell — "The Speech I Couldn't Give," *Campus Life*, June/July 2002.

Rone Tempest — "Claims of Political Harassment Turn Teen into Conservative Hero," *Seattle Times*, January 23, 2004.

Kate Zernike — "Free Speech Ruling Voids School District's Harassment Policy," *New York Times*, February 16, 2001.

CHAPTER 3

Should Schools Be Allowed to Infringe on Students' Right to Privacy?

Chapter Preface

On a Friday in 2003, a group of thirteen- and fourteen-year-old students at Intermediate School (I.S.) 164 in New York skipped class to attend a party that reportedly involved sexual activity. When they returned to school on Monday, the female students were questioned about their sexual history by school officials and suspended until they brought proof that they had undergone gynecological exams and tests for pregnancy and sexually transmitted diseases (STDs). The male students were apparently not reprimanded. When two girls brought doctors' notes stating that they had been seen, administrators allegedly told them to produce documentation indicating the results of the tests.

Although the New York Civil Liberties Union publicized the incident at I.S. 164 as an unnecessary privacy violation by school officials, administrators would likely claim that they wanted to identify any harmful health conditions as early as possible to protect the girls and the student body. This case illustrates the complexity of privacy rights in school. School officials attempt to fulfill their duties to protect students and maintain a safe educational environment while rights advocates assert that students' privacy must be respected.

In an earlier and similar case a high school swim coach, Michael Seip, and others suspected that swim team member Leah Gruenke was pregnant. After she denied ever having sex, the coach either persuaded or intimidated her into taking a home pregnancy test. The coach was later advised that swimming during pregnancy was not harmful. Eventually a court ruled in *Gruenke v. Seip* that the school did not have justification for requiring the test and thus invading the girl's privacy because swimming did not endanger the student or the fetus.

In light of the 2000 *Gruenke* decision, the New York Civil Liberties Union filed a federal lawsuit against I.S. 164 principal Lavern Reid, another administrator, the Department of Education, and the City of New York. Claiming that the girls' rights to privacy, bodily integrity, equality, and due process had been violated when officials asked the girls to produce documentation of their gynecological exams and pregnancy tests, the suit sought $200,000 for each student. The forced tests and suspensions "reflected a fundamental indifference to the rights of the girls," said Donna Lieberman, the union's executive director.

Lieberman conceded that Principal Reid had good intentions; in fact, few people doubted this. Reid and other administrators apparently felt that the students' truancy and possible sexual activity at such a young age deserved extreme disciplinary action. New York Schools chancellor Joel Klein reminded reporters, "As in any lawsuit, there are two sides. Different people have different views of what happened and we will respond appropriately in court." Many did question the school's reasoning, however. *New York Times* writer Alan Feuer claimed that the medical tests were issued "instead of giving the girls detentions, demerits or some other common form of punishment." Members of the community were concerned, believing the school would have punished the girls if their test results had been positive.

Eventually the girls agreed to drop their lawsuit, as long as the school district changed its policy concerning the medical testing of students. Now school officials may not demand that students undergo pregnancy, STD, or HIV testing, nor can they make students reveal whether they are pregnant or infected with a disease. One of the teenage plaintiffs in the case declared, "I'm really glad that they're changing the rules and training the principals so they know what the rules are. . . . It means that other kids aren't going to have to go through the same thing I did and feel bad like I did. It was so embarrassing and made me feel small."

The settlement in the I.S. 164 case confirms that administrators may not ask students to leave school for being pregnant or having an STD. More importantly, many analysts contend, this case reaffirms students' rights to privacy. The medical privacy rights of students is just one topic examined in the following chapter, in which several authors debate whether student privacy rights can and should be waived.

> *"Students learn government may search*
> *without cause, individualized suspicion, or*
> *apparent purpose. . . . (Publicly educated)*
> *Americans may deem it 'reasonable' to*
> *waive privacy protections for many*
> *purposes."*

Random School Searches Undermine Students' Privacy Rights

Joe Blankenau and Mark Leeper

In the following viewpoint Joe Blankenau and Mark Leeper contend that random school search policies are meant to promote authorities' morals, model their ideas that behavior such as drug use is sinful, and exert their authority over students. Ignoring the fact that random searches are ineffective, policy makers and principals overstate the dangers that drugs pose to students to justify pointless searches, Blankenau and Leeper assert. Suspicionless search policies, they claim, teach students that privacy rights are unimportant and that it is reasonable to waive constitutional rights. Joe Blankenau and Mark Leeper are associate professors of political science at Wayne State College in Nebraska.

As you read, consider the following questions:
1. According to Blankenau and Leeper, what three student "deficiencies" enhance a principal's power?
2. Name the three reasons the authors give for their belief that random searching of schools will increase.

Joe Blankenau and Mark Leeper, "Public School Search Policies and the 'Politics of Sin,'" *Policy Studies Journal*, vol. 31, November 2003, pp. 565–85. Copyright © 2003 by the Policy Studies Organization. Reproduced by permission of Blackwell Publishers, Ltd.

A re public high schools adopting aggressive search poli-cies with greater frequency? If so, why? This study describes and analyzes the presence of random, suspicionless drug searches in the Nebraska public schools. The adoption, effectiveness, and impact of random school searches (as reported by public school principals) is considered and critiqued through the theoretical lens of "morality politics.". . .

Morality Policy Deals with Basic Values

Morality politics involves conflict over the authoritative legitimatization of one set of rights or values over another. The debate generated by morality politics is one . . . in which "at least one advocacy coalition . . . portrays the issue in terms of morality or sin and uses moral arguments in its policy advocacy" [according to research in the *Policy Studies Journal*].

When government takes a position and generates morality policy, the imprimatur of the state is squarely stamped on one set of mores or values. Government, therefore, has great power to "define, legitimize, and reconcile disparate world views," [writes author P.B.] Heymann, and can greatly enhance the social status of some groups and reduce the status of others. The values under question are usually related to the demand for, and the desire to consume, what some people see as "sin" (e.g., pornography, abortion, gambling, alcohol, and drugs).

Morality policy process and outputs differ from other types of public policy. First, morality policy involves principles with sensitive moral undertones, leading to conflict over fundamental values not readily resolved through deliberation. Rather than the political system engaging in sterile policy analysis to determine the best path to take for an agreed upon policy goal, debate spins around the often explosive, emotion-laden values the system should embrace.

Second, because morality policy deals with basic values, it is much easier to understand for all actors, and so morality policy tends to avoid laborious and potentially arcane issues of policy analysis. As such, morality policy is highly salient and easily accessible to the public, and therefore enjoys a "technical simplicity" that invites widespread participation. The public's interest may be piqued by an overriding sense their basic values are being threatened, thus exacerbating alarm and promoting a dualistic, black-and-white, "us-against-them" policy approach. As a consequence, morality policy sometimes invites a racial bias in application. [Policy studies expert Kenneth J.] Meier notes that morality policy is disproportionately targeted at minorities and immigrants. Morality policy, in sum, typically invites more interest, albeit an emotive, reflexive, sometimes prejudiced response devoid of prolonged, substantive discussion.

Morality Policy Is Expressive, Not Results-Driven

Third, the individual actors involved in morality policy overstate the need for governmental response. The general public tends to overstate their actual desire to curtail sin, masking and compensating for their own minor peccadilloes. Politicians and policymakers also tend to overestimate or overlook the actual presence of the problem. Bureaucrats, as a result, are given wide discretion and ample room to contend with the threat and will coincidentally seek greater resources and more extreme policies to justify and sustain the need for their bureaucracy. Under these circumstances, it is hard to imagine any effective resistance to the ratcheting upward response to the perceived sin.

Fourth, morality policy reflects a more expressive policy approach, as opposed to an instrumental, results-driven approach. Since the mission is to make a point, not to generate concrete outcomes, such policies are adopted with greater frequency regardless of any data or proof that the policies work. Meier argues that such policies gain momentum and acceptance despite a near certainty they will fail in any quantifiable, assessable sense.

Last, morality policy, being steeped in accepted values, tends to subordinate or abase competing sets of rights. Other sets of values, less imbued with morality (e.g., constitutional safeguards) will fall by the wayside as the sin is addressed.

Because morality policy tends to be the product of unvarnished majority rule, individuals in the minority are exposed to the potential of greater harassment, oppression, and government-sponsored searching. Constitutional barriers to government activity (and their underlying logic) erode as the desire to thwart sin intensifies. Without the presence of an insulated, attentive state or federal court system, the dynamics of morality politics can quickly push aside First, Fourth, and Fourteenth Amendment rights.

Morality Policy in Public Schools

Morality policy in the context of public schools is an increasingly important, yet relatively unexamined, field of study. Government policies that are implemented within schools—particularly policies infused with morality—are likely to have an impact well beyond the immediate, tangible policy goal and the targeted sin.

According to [political scientist Sandra] Vergari, public schools

> play an important role not only in helping students to acquire knowledge and develop technical skills, but also in socializing students according to the norms and mores of society. The moral values expressed and enforced by the schools can be interpreted as expected values for all members of society.

Thus, if the state implements morality policy in schools, it is using the school as a domain to ferret out sinful behaviors, inculcating students with state-sponsored values, and perhaps even teaching students a forceful lesson in values that may promote morality but erode citizenship. If the state chooses the public school as a primary front to wage war on sin, the battle may leave an indelible mark on the students' sense of themselves, their rights, and the propriety of government intrusion.

The central government actor in this morality politics play (i.e., random drug searches) is the high school principal. [Politics researcher Christopher Z.] Mooney notes that most of the work on morality policy has looked at states as the unit of analysis. However, policymaking is strongly influenced by individual bureaucrats. Therefore, Mooney suggests that "issues for future study include the role of the bureaucracy in forming and implementing morality policy."

In the realm of school drug searches, the role of principals—their attitudes, perceptions and behaviors—are vital in understanding the logic and presence of these policies. Although school boards may pronounce the broad policies regarding drug searches, and superintendents and their staff may provide resources or oversight, principals affect policymaking through their informational roles and their actual implementation of drug policies in the hallways and cafeterias. Further, school boards have become much less effective in providing policy oversight, given the increasing complexity of education policy and the increase in activity from other actors.

The Principal's Power Is Strengthened by Students' Vulnerability

The power and policy discretion of principals is also enhanced by their unique position in the school and the nature of those whom they administer. According to [an article in *Theory Into Practice* by C.] Marshall, public school administrators are "street-level bureaucrats" who work directly with the public and have considerable discretion and ample decision-making authority. The autonomy and power of the street-level bureaucrat is enabled and enhanced by having clients that lack the "knowledge, legitimacy, or ability to call them to task."

In the school environment, the clients (students) hold all three of these deficiencies. Students are, at best, only dimly aware of constitutional safeguards, and they lack the intellectual maturity to understand the nuances of Fourth Amendment jurisprudence. Authoritative statements can swiftly rebuff any objection to intrusions on their privacy, for example, "we need to keep the school safe," "it's not your locker," and "if you don't have drugs, you have nothing to worry about."

Further, students' legitimacy and ability to hold school administrators accountable for their actions are undermined significantly by their age. They are minors and thus are not generally deemed capable of making decisions about their conduct, such as whether or not they choose to drink alcohol or drive automobiles. More important, they are perceived as children—vulnerable and in need of protection—in the eyes of the school, public, and government. According to Meier, this can be problematic, as "children are a positive social construction; and dangers to children, however rare, can often justify more extreme policies."

The principal, then, assumes a multifaceted role that includes serving as guardian or protector of the child (*in loco parentis*). Most children are led to believe, through hard experience, that the Constitution, its Bill of Rights, and plain reason are not necessarily safeguards against the vicissitudes of parental discipline. Principals who perceive and portray themselves as de facto "parents" likely shield themselves from the challenges and resistance that the actions of pure public officials would generate.

Survey Responses of Nebraska High School Principals

How Successful Have Your Drug Policies Been?
(In percentages)

Level of success	In reducing drug use	In finding drug violators
None	12.8	16.4
Somewhat	55.8	50.3
Moderately	26.7	31.6
Extremely	4.7	1.8
Total	100.0	100.1*

*rounding error.

Threats to Student Rights and Level of Student Resistance?
(In percentages)

	Level of threat	Level of resistance
None	89.2	54.2
A small amount	9.1	35.7
Moderately	1.1	9.5
A great deal	0.6	0.6
Total	100.0	100.0

Joe Blankenau and Mark Leeper, *Policy Studies Journal*, November 2003.

Principals as street-level bureaucrats hold substantial power and a unique brand of authority. Students, perceived as immature, vulnerable, and unemancipated, are at a disadvantage in checking or challenging this power. The attitudes, perceptions, and insights of principals regarding random school searches are critical because of their unique role in the public school system. They are there to witness and report the presence of searches, and their discretion and authority affect the scope and impact of searches on public school children. . . .

Morality Policy Applied to Nebraska School Searches

Nebraska public school students are subjected to greater levels of intrusion than prior cohorts. Critics and civil libertarians would argue this augmented search activity emerged despite the fact [that] (1) only 1 in 10 Nebraska principals describe their school's drug problem as "serious" or "severe," (2) fewer than 1 in 5 Nebraska high school students report coming in contact with drugs on school grounds, (3) principals uniformly report the drug problem is significantly less severe in the school than in the surrounding community or nation, and (4) principals admit the searching is relatively ineffective in ferreting out drug use and finding perpetrators.

Searching in the Nebraska public schools thus reflects some of the features of morality policy—the policies invite pressure and participation from multifarious local sources; the searching increases where there are larger concentrations of racial minorities; and the policies gain momentum and acceptance despite any tangible proof of need or effectiveness.

It is unlikely that court, concerned parents, or principals will clamor for teen privacy and student rights. Rather, the current legal and cultural landscape provide fertile ground for increased random searching. First, most courts currently view the general interest of the state (i.e., protecting our nation's children from drugs) as overcoming any student privacy rights. The Fourth Amendment, after all, prohibits random, suspicionless searches that are unreasonable. The government, therefore, has ample room to subjectively identify reasonable, generic "special needs" that supercede individual privacy interests.

Protecting our nation's children from drugs is readily accepted as such a "special need." Courts have gradually abandoned the notion, articulated in *New Jersey v. T.L.O.* (1985), that a student must invite suspicion before a constitutional search may be conducted. Today, random searches of specific students in remote schools, without cause, are deemed "reasonable" and constitutionally permissible to address this undifferentiated national trend (the "epidemic of drugs") regardless of conditions in the specific school. Justice Clarence Thomas, author of the majority opinion in *Pottawatomie v. Earls* (2002), argued "the nationwide drug epidemic makes the war against drugs a pressing problem in every school." Even if there is no clear and present drug use in a particular school, Thomas wrote, "the need to prevent and deter the substantial harm of childhood drug use provides the necessary immediacy for a school testing policy."

Of course, Nebraska principals report random searches in schools are not particularly effective in dealing with drugs. Thus, the largely symbolic presence of morality policy (school searches) steadily grows despite any perceived practical effect, and our nation's highest court allows for the abasement of competing rights (the Fourth Amendment) because of its assumed preventive effect.

Supreme Court Decisions Favor Protecting Students over Protecting Their Rights

Supreme Court justices are often asked to select from and balance competing sets of values articulated within the Constitution. Although promoting safety and order over individual freedom is a perfectly legitimate path, the Court's blanket approval of preemptive searching does not go unnoticed by principals and reduces concerns regarding intrusive drug policies.

Second, our nation's parents are quite comfortable with this appraisal of the Fourth Amendment and student rights. In the precedent setting case *Veronia v. Acton* (1995) (which validated random urine testing for public school athletes), parents unanimously approved of the school's proposal at a local meeting. In *Pottawatomie v. Earls* (2002) (regarding a rural Oklahoma school district's policy demanding random urine tests of all students engaged in extracurricular activities), Justice Stephen Breyer—commonly labeled a "liberal"—expressed at oral argument that he, as a parent, hoped schools would do all within their power to protect his children from drugs. In his concurring opinion, Justice Breyer wrote he was comfortable with random drug testing if "the school board provides an opportunity for the airing of differences at public meetings designed to give the entire community the opportunity" to evaluate and develop the drug policy. Again, morality policy is noted for its accessibility and simplicity, not for its rational appraisal of policy efficacy. It's hard to imagine that "public meetings" would provide any brake to the concerned majority or the flow of morality policy.

Third, federal courts are frequently adopting the position (starting with *Vernonia*) that children are firmly in the custody of the state (*in loco parentis*). Students thus enjoy few rights of privacy in the face of principal-as-parent, and based on the written comments of Nebraska's principals, students should expect little sympathy from those controlling policy on school grounds. Principal support of random searching was nearly universal and fell into three general categories: (1) that students forfeit rights when they engage in wrongdoing; (2) that the overarching need for safety overcomes any individual rights; and (3) the policies are clearly written and widely promulgated. In addition, principals regularly expressed frustration that parents and law enforcement clamor for "something to be done" but abdicate responsibility to the school. The loneliness and pressure stemming from these demands clearly pushes principals to become more aggressive without careful consideration of efficacy or consequences.

Suspicionless Searches Teach Students That Rights Do Not Matter

But, why is this important? Before principals, courts, and parents agree to suspend Fourth Amendment rights on school grounds, one must remember the special nature of the public school. Although it is a government enterprise, the primary mission of the school is to educate our nation's children. The government interest in promoting safety and morality on school grounds is indeed immense, but one must be careful to note the indirect, almost imperceptible lessons that are provided when schools become the venue to wage the war on drugs. If a urine test, and a locker search, and a breathalyzer, and a dog sniff become a right of passage within high schools, students learn government may search without cause, individualized suspicion, or apparent purpose. And because the Fourth Amendment is a subjective protection, a generation of (publicly educated) Americans may deem it "reasonable" to waive privacy protections for many purposes (e.g., a war on drugs or a war on terror).

Future studies should continue to monitor the presence of random searches in the school context and attempt to measure their effects on public school children. Do increased levels of searches significantly alter students' perceptions of themselves, the government, and their inherent rights? This should be understood before we, as a society, continue to allow the momentum of morality politics to flow in the public school.

"A student's right to privacy gives way to a school's duty to maintain a safe environment."

Random School Searches Ensure Safety and Are Constitutional

Mitchell L. Yell and Michael E. Rozalski

In the following viewpoint Mitchell L. Yell and Michael E. Rozalski contend that students' privacy rights sometimes must be waived so that schools can maintain a safe, orderly environment. They review the necessity and legality of random school search policies and conclude that because students have fewer rights than adults, administrators can search their lockers and backpacks if they have reasonable suspicion of illegal activity. Although courts favor the schools' duties over students' privacy interests, students are protected from unreasonable searches, according to Yell and Rozalski. Mitchell L. Yell is an associate professor and Michael E. Rozalski is a doctoral student in Programs in Special Education at the University of South Carolina.

As you read, consider the following questions:
1. Describe the two-part test that the Court adopted as a result of *New Jersey v. T.L.O.*
2. What example does the viewpoint provide to illustrate an unreasonable strip search?
3. According to the authors, what class of procedures normally does not require reasonable suspicion, and why don't authorities have to satisfy that requirement?

Mitchell L. Yell and Michael E. Rozalski, "Searching for Safe Schools: Legal Issues in the Prevention of School Violence," *Journal of Emotional and Behavioral Disorders*, Fall 2000. Copyright © 2000 by Pro-Ed. Reproduced by permission.

The high court has recognized that schools have a duty to educate students in a safe and orderly environment. In [its] decisions, the Court has attempted to balance the rights of students with the duties of school district personnel. For example, a student's freedom of expression is limited to expression or speech that does not interfere with the school's operation, precisely because schools have a duty to establish standards of student conduct and behavior. Similarly, a student's right to privacy gives way to a school's duty to maintain a safe environment.

The two Supreme Court decisions that directly affect how school officials may keep schools safe and orderly while safeguarding the rights of students are *New Jersey v. T.L.O.* (1985) and *Veronia School District v. Acton* (1995). In fact, [school safety expert Bernard] James referred to the decision in *New Jersey v. T.L.O.* as a virtual blueprint for designing school safety policies. In this case, the Court noted that the interests of teachers and administrators in maintaining discipline in the classroom would be furthered by a less restrictive rule of law that would balance schoolchildren's legitimate expectations of privacy and the school's equally legitimate need to maintain an environment in which learning could take place. We now discuss these very important cases.

New Jersey v. T.L.O.

In 1985, the U.S. Supreme Court in *New Jersey v. T.L.O.* (hereafter *TLO*) addressed warrantless searches in the schools. A teacher in a New Jersey high school discovered two girls smoking in the school lavatory. The students were taken to the vice-principal's office. The vice-principal took a purse from one of the girls to examine it for cigarettes. In addition to the cigarettes, the purse also contained cigarette-rolling papers. Suspecting that the girl might have marijuana, the vice-principal emptied the contents of the purse. In it he found a pipe, a small amount of marijuana, a large amount of money in small bills, a list of people owing TLO money, and two letters implicating her in marijuana dealing. The girl's parents were called, and the evidence was turned over to police. Charges were brought by the police, and based on the evidence collected by the vice-principal and TLO's confession, a juvenile court in New Jersey declared TLO delinquent. The parents appealed the decision on the grounds that the search was conducted without a warrant and, therefore, illegal under the Fourth Amendment. Because the search was conducted illegally, the parents argued, the evidence was inadmissible. The case went to the New Jersey Supreme Court, which reversed the decision of the juvenile court and ordered the evidence obtained during the vice-principal's search suppressed on the grounds that the warrantless search was unconstitutional.

The U.S. Supreme Court eventually heard the case. The Court declared that the Fourth Amendment, prohibiting illegal searches and seizures, applied to students as well as adults. The Court also noted, however, that a student's privacy interests must be weighed against the need of administrators and teachers to maintain order and discipline in schools. Furthermore, the Court noted that maintaining security and order in schools required some easing of the requirements normally imposed on police.

The Court ruled that schools did not need to obtain a search warrant before searching a student; however, the Fourth Amendment's reasonableness standard, a standard lower than that of probable cause, had to be satisfied. Probable cause refers to a standard to which police are held; that is, police may only conduct a search if it is more than probable that the search will reveal evidence of illegal activities. Based on this standard, police must usually obtain a warrant prior to conducting the search. The reasonableness standard that school officials must meet holds that a reasonable person would have cause to suspect that evidence of illegal activities be present before conducting the search. If these preconditions are met, school officials may conduct the search. The reasonableness standard is much easier to meet than is the standard of probable cause.

The Court also adopted a two-part test to determine whether a search conducted by school officials was reasonable and, therefore, constitutionally valid. The two parts of this test that must be satisfied are that the search must be (a) justified at inception and (b) related to violations of school rules or policies. First, the search must be conducted as the result of a legitimate suspicion. This does not mean that school officials must be absolutely certain prior to conducting a search, but rather that there is a commonsense probability regarding the necessity of a search. A search cannot be justified on the basis of what was found during the search. Situations that justify a reasonable suspicion include information from student informers, police tips, anonymous tips and phone calls, and unusual student conduct. Second, the scope of the search must be reasonably related to the rule violation that led to the search in the first place. Because the vice-principal's search of TLO met the Supreme Court's test, it reversed the judgment of the New Jersey Supreme Court and ruled that the marijuana was admissible as evidence.

Veronia School District v. Acton

A school district in Oregon was experiencing a startling increase in drug use, rebelliousness, and disciplinary problems among its students. School officials identified student athletes as the ring-leaders in the drug problem. Following unsuccessful attempts at solving the problem through the use of educational programs, a public meeting was held. During the meeting, school officials received unanimous parent support for adopting a drug-testing program for all students participating in sports. The policy required that if a student wanted to participate in interscholastic sports, the student and his or her parents had to sign a consent form submitting to drug testing. If a student and his or her parents did not sign the consent form, the student was not allowed to participate in sports. A seventh-grade student, James Acton, who wanted to play interscholastic football, refused to sign the consent form. When the school did not allow James to play football, his parents sued the school district, alleging that their son's constitutional rights had been violated. The case, *Veronia School District v. Acton* (hereafter *Veronia*) was heard by the U.S. Supreme Court in 1995. In a six to three decision, the high court ruled in favor of the school district's drug-testing policy. Although the Court's ruling only addressed drug testing of student athletes, the decision has important implications for school districts' search and seizure policies. The Court, citing its decision in *TLO*, stated that the Fourth Amendment to the Constitution required bal-

Factors Justifying a Student Search

Factors Generally Sufficient by Themselves
- A crime or school rule violation is observed in progress.
- A weapon or portion of weapon is observed on a student.
- A student has told others that he or she has a weapon on campus.
- A student has been seen in possession of illegal items.
- A student has been seen in possession of stolen items.
- A student is found with incriminating items.
- The smell of burning tobacco or marijuana is detected.
- A student appears to be under the influence of alcohol or drugs.
- A student admits to committing a crime or school rule violation.
- A student fits a *detailed* or *unusual* description of suspect of recently reported crime or school rule violation.
- A student provides *specific* incriminating evidence against another student.
- An emergency situation exists where school official can provide immediate assistance to avoid serious injury if a student search is conducted.
- A student provides oral or written *voluntary* consent to conduct a search.

Factors Generally Not Sufficient by Themselves
- A student flees from the vicinity of recent crime or school rule violation.
- A student flees upon the approach of a school official.
- Imprecise information about a crime or school rule violation has been provided to school officials.
- A student threatens others with words or behavior without an indication that the student possesses a weapon (a reasonable indication that a student possesses a weapon always provides *reasonable suspicion* justifying a search).
- A student has a history of previous similar criminal or school rule violations.
- A report has been made of a stolen item, including a description and value of the item and place from which it was stolen.
- A student was seen leaving an area where crimes or school rule violations are often committed.
- A student became unduly nervous or excited when approached by a school official.
- A student made a suspicious movement.

Office of the Attorney General, *School Search Manual*, 2004.

ancing the interests of the student's privacy and the school district's legitimate interest in preserving order and safety. In making this determination, the Court noted that students in school have a decreased expectation of privacy relative to adults in the general population. The Court also considered the relative unobtrusiveness of the drug-testing policy. The primary consideration, therefore, was regarding the special context of public schools, which act as guardians and tutors of the students in their care. Clearly, this decision indicated that in situations involving such preventive measures, courts will favor the needs of the school over the privacy interests of students when the procedures used are reasonable.

Maintaining Safe Schools Is of Utmost Importance

The *TLO* and *Veronia* decisions affirmed the constitutional rights of students to be free of unreasonable searches and seizures and to possess a reasonable expectation of privacy while at school. In both cases, however, the Court granted a great deal of latitude to schools because they have a legitimate duty to educate students in a safe and orderly environment. The high court clearly stated that when the rights of students and those of school officials seem to conflict, the law favors the duties of school officials.

According to the *TLO* decision, the law permits educators to respond to school safety problems as the situation dictates, providing the actions are reasonable. In *Veronia*, the high court noted that the privacy expectations of students in public schools are less than those of the general public because school authorities act in loco parentis. In loco parentis is a concept that originated in English common law. According to this concept, when parents place their children in schools, they give a certain amount of their control of their children to school personnel. The principal and teacher, therefore, have the authority to teach, guide, correct, and discipline children to achieve educational objectives.

Factors That School Personnel Must Consider

Nonetheless, these decisions do place some degree of restraint on school personnel. In *TLO* the Court held that reasonable grounds must exist to lead school authorities to believe a search is necessary, and the search must be related to the original suspicion. According to [authors John H.] Dise, [Chitra S.] Iyer, and [Jeffrey J.] Noorman, this standard requires that school officials weigh the credibility of the information prior to making a decision to conduct a search. Court decisions following *TLO* have recognized situations in which searches and seizures in school environments do not give rise to Fourth Amendment concerns (i.e., searches during which even the standard of reasonable suspicion is not required). These situations include searches (a) to which a student voluntarily consents, (b) of material left in view of the school authorities, (c) in an emergency to prevent injury or property damage, (d) by police authorities that are incidental to arrests, and (e) of lost property.

The intrusiveness of the search is also a relevant factor. Considering the nature of the possible offense, the search should not be overly intrusive (e.g., a strip search to locate missing money). When these conditions are met, school officials have a great deal of leeway in conducting searches of students and their property.

In *Veronia*, the Court stated that the interest of the school in taking the action (e.g., random searches, drug tests) must be important enough to justify the procedure. The Court saw protecting students from drug use and maintaining a safe and orderly educational environment as "important—indeed compelling."

These decisions are extremely important because they give school officials guidance in using procedures such as targeted and random searches, drug testing, and surveillance. . . .

Targeted Searches of Students' Property

Although the U.S. Supreme Court has not heard a case involving targeted searches of student property, the Court did uphold searches of government offices, desks, and file cabinets based on reasonable suspicion (*O'Connor v. Ortega*, 1987). Lower courts, using this decision as precedent, have upheld school officials' targeted or random searches of student lockers, if the searches are based on reasonable suspicion (*In the Interest of Isaiah B.*, 1993; *People v. Overton*, 1969). Searches by school authorities may also extend to students' cars and locked briefcases (*State of Washington v. Slattery*, 1990), as well as objects in which contraband may be hidden, such as backpacks (*People v. Dilworth*, 1996).

When school officials use tertiary prevention procedures, such as targeted searches of students and their property, they do not have to wait until the illegal behavior affects the school before taking action. School officials are legally permitted to act in response to reasonable suspicion that a student is violating or may have violated school rules or committed an illegal act. That is, they only need reason to believe that the safety or order of the school environment may be threatened by student behavior.

There is, however, another class of procedures that in many situations do not require reasonable suspicion prior to being undertaken. We refer to these as secondary procedures. Secondary procedures include random searches, use of metal detectors, and surveillance. It is legally useful to consider such searches separately from targeted searches and other tertiary procedures because the standard that school officials must meet in using secondary procedures is lower. In the next section, we briefly examine the legality of secondary prevention procedures when used by school officials.

Random, Suspicionless Searches Are Legal

Secondary prevention procedures involve school officials' attempts to seize weapons or contraband materials before they can be used. These procedures typically consist of random searches of students' belongings or property (e.g., lockers, automobiles, desks, backpacks). The use of metal detectors and various means of surveillance also fall into this category. Furthermore, the use of metal detectors to search students, even though there is no suspicion or consent to a search, is permitted (*Illinois v. Pruitt*, 1996). To keep weapons, drugs, and contraband off school property, random searches of students and their property are now common occurrences in public schools, especially at the secondary level. Secondary procedures, like tertiary procedures, are governed by the Fourth Amendment to the U.S. Constitution, which prohibits unreasonable searches and seizures. Unlike tertiary procedures, secondary procedures are directed at all students or are conducted randomly and therefore do not require reasonable suspicion.

A decision that has great importance for school districts conducting random searches was *In the Interest of Isaiah B.* (hereafter *Isaiah B.*, 1993). In this decision, the Wisconsin Supreme Court ruled that a student did not have reasonable expectations of privacy in his school locker. The court based its decision largely on the existence of the Milwaukee Public Schools policy regarding student lockers. According to the school policy,

> School lockers are the property of Milwaukee Public Schools. At no time does the Milwaukee School District relinquish its exclusive control of lockers provided for the convenience of students. School authorities for any reason may conduct periodic general inspections of lockers at any time without notice, without student consent, and without a search warrant.

Unless prohibited by state law, [B.] Miller and [W.C.] Ahrbecker suggested [in "Legal Issues and School Violence"] that schools develop policies regarding locker searches, such as the Milwaukee Public Schools policy, that notify students and parents that there is no reasonable expectation of privacy in a student locker and that both random and targeted searches of the locker may be conducted without student or parental consent. [Educational law expert Eugene C.] Bjorklun, likewise, concluded that random locker searches may be conducted without individualized suspicion.

Random Searches Serve as a Deterrent

Secondary procedures include the use of random searches, surveillance cameras, and metal detectors. These procedures are legally proactive because they serve as a deterrent. School officials attempt to seize contraband and weapons before they are used. Unlike tertiary procedures, the *TLO* standard of reasonable suspicion is not as directly applicable in situations involving random property searches and other secondary procedures. That is, school officials do not necessarily need reasonable suspicion to conduct, for example, random locker checks. Rather, school officials must balance their legitimate need to search lockers with the privacy rights of students. When conducting searches of students and their property, it is important that school district officials adhere to established guidelines and policies that correspond with the case law. Students have diminished expectations of privacy while at school; nevertheless, school officials must notify students and their parents that student property may be subjected to random searches and that surveillance measures will be used and that the purpose of such measures is to ensure that students are educated in a safe and orderly environment.

"[Court] decisions support minors' right to receive contraception without parental consent."

Students Have the Right to Receive Family Planning Services Without Parental Notification

Abigail English and Carol A. Ford

In the following viewpoint Abigail English and Carol A. Ford assert that requirements that parents be notified when their teens request family planning information from community or school health clinics infringe on students' privacy rights. Moreover, they argue that requiring parental notification prevents teens from seeking care and from openly communicating with doctors, thereby threatening students' health. Abigail English is director of the Center for Adolescent Health & the Law. Carol A. Ford is associate professor in the departments of pediatrics and internal medicine at the University of North Carolina, Chapel Hill.

As you read, consider the following questions:
1. Under what circumstances may a minor be considered his or her own personal representative, according to the viewpoint?
2. In English's and Ford's contention, how do parents consent to their children's health care in school-based health centers?

Abigail English and Carol A. Ford, "The HIPAA Privacy Rule and Adolescents: Legal Questions and Clinical Challenges," *Perspectives on Sexual and Reproductive Health*, vol. 36, March/April 2004. Copyright © 2004 by the Alan Guttmacher Institute. Reproduced by permission.

In August 2002, a new federal rule took effect that protects the privacy of individuals' health information and medical records. The rule, which is based on requirements contained in the Health Insurance Portability and Accountability Act of 1996 (HIPAA), embodies important protections for minors, along with a significant degree of deference to other laws (both state and federal) and to the judgment of health care providers. These provisions represent a compromise between competing viewpoints about the importance of parental access to minors' health information and the availability of confidential adolescent health care services.

Confidential Health Care for Adolescents Is Necessary

Over the past several decades, adolescents have gained many opportunities to receive confidential health care services, particularly for concerns related to sexual activity, pregnancy, HIV and other sexually transmitted diseases (STDs), substance abuse and mental health. From both a clinical and a public policy perspective, protection of confidentiality for adolescents has been based on recognition that some minors would not seek needed health care if they could not receive it confidentially, and that their forgoing care would have negative health implications for them as well as society.

Concerns about privacy can prevent adolescents from seeking care. In two large nationally representative surveys, approximately a quarter of middle and high school students reported having forgone health care they needed. In one of these, a third of students who did not seek care reported that one of their reasons was "not wanting to tell their parents." The impact of privacy concerns when adolescents require specific services to address sensitive health issues is likely much higher. For example, half of single, sexually active females younger than 18 years surveyed in family planning clinics in Wisconsin reported that they would stop using the clinics if parental notification for prescription contraceptives were mandatory; another one in 10 reported that they would delay or discontinue use of specific services, such as services for STDs. Furthermore, only 1% of adolescent girls who indicated they would stop using family planning services reported that they would also stop having intercourse; the vast majority reported that they would continue to have sex, but use less effective contraceptive methods or none at all.

Privacy concerns also influence where adolescents go for health care, can deter them from communicating openly with providers, and can make them reluctant to accept services such as pelvic examinations and testing for STDs. Confidentiality protections for adolescent health care are reflected in the policies and ethical guidelines of a wide range of medical and health care professional organizations. They also are embodied in numerous state and federal laws that have great significance for the application of the HIPAA privacy rule to adolescents' health information.

Provisions of the HIPAA Privacy Rule

The HIPAA privacy rule creates new rights for individuals to have access to their health information and medical records (referred to as "protected health information"), to obtain copies and to request corrections. It also specifies when an individual's authorization is required for disclosure of protected health information; authorization is generally not required for the use of the information and its disclosure for the purpose of treatment, payment or health care operations. The rule applies to health plans, health care providers [including most school-based health clinics] and health care clearinghouses (which are all "covered entities"). The vast majority of health care professionals who provide care to adolescents are required to comply.

Under the HIPAA privacy rule, adolescents who legally are adults (aged 18 or older) and emancipated minors can exercise the rights of individuals; specific provisions address the protected health information of adolescents who are younger than 18 and not emancipated. Parents (including guardians and persons acting in loco parentis) are considered to be the "personal representatives" of their unemancipated minor children if they have the right to make health care decisions for them. As personal representatives, parents generally have access to their children's protected health information. In specific circumstances, however, parents may not be the personal representatives of their minor children.

Minors Have the Right to Consent to Health Care

A minor is considered "the individual" who can exercise rights under the rule in one of three circumstances. The first situation—and the one that is likely to occur most often—is when the minor has the right to consent to health care and has consented, such as when a minor has consented to treatment of an STD under a state minor consent law. The second situation is when the minor may legally receive the care without parental consent, and the minor or another individual or a court has consented to the care, such as when a minor has requested and received court approval to have an abortion without parental consent or notification. The third situation is when a parent has assented to an agreement of confidentiality between the health care provider and the minor, which occurs most often when an adolescent is seen by a physician who knows the family. In each of these circumstances, the parent is not the personal representative of the minor and does not automatically have the right of access to health information specific to the situation, unless the minor requests that the parent act as the personal representative and have access. . . .

Every state has laws that allow minors to give their own consent for some kinds of health care—including emergency, general health, contraceptive, pregnancy-related, HIV or other STD, substance abuse and mental health care. Every state also has some laws that allow minors to consent for care if they are emancipated, mature, living apart from their parents, pregnant, parents, high school graduates or older than a certain age. Many of these laws have been in place for several decades. The HIPAA privacy rule defers to them.

Adolescents and the professionals who provide their health care have long expected that when an adolescent is allowed to give consent for health care, information pertaining to it will usually be considered confidential. The language of the statutes themselves sometimes supports this understanding. Many minor consent laws contain explicit provisions regarding the disclosure of information to parents. Some do not allow disclosure without the minor's permission. Others leave the decision about disclosure to the physician's discretion. Very few mandate disclosure. Some minor consent laws are silent on the question of parents' access to the information. In those cases, unless state or other law addresses parents' access, the HIPAA rule gives discretion to the provider or health plan to decide whether a parent who requests access should have it; the decision must be made by a licensed health care professional.

A Threat to Teens' Health

In *Carey v. Population Services International*, the Supreme Court ruled that minors have the right to access family planning services without unjustified parental or governmental intervention. Organized medicine and state lawmakers also recognize that laws mandating parental involvement actually harm the teens and families they purport to protest. . . .

Studies demonstrate that requiring parental consent or notification for family planning services will cause many teens—fearing abuse, punishment or parental disappointment—to delay or avoid needed medical care. . . .

In the year following the elimination of a parental consent requirement for HIV testing in Connecticut, the number of teens aged 13-17 obtaining HIV tests at publicly funded facilities doubled.

Fifty-eight (58) percent of high school students surveyed in three public schools in Massachusetts reported having health concerns that they did not want to share with their parents. Approximately 25 percent of the students said they would forgo medical treatment if disclosure of treatment to their parents were a possibility.

NARAL Pro-Choice America Foundation, "Government-Mandated Parental Involvement in Family Planning Services Threatens Health," January 1, 2004. www.naral.org.

For adults, the HIPAA privacy rule defers to state laws that provide stronger privacy protections than the federal rule, but if state laws provide weaker protection, the federal rule controls. For minors, on the question of parental access to information, the rule defers to state laws unless they are silent or unclear. Many states have enacted laws concerning privacy of health information and medical records, although not all address disclosure of information to parents when minors have consented to the care. At least three states—California, Montana and Washington—have adopted health privacy laws that explicitly give minors authority over their own information and records when they have the legal right to consent to care.

HIPAA Protects School-Based Health Center Records

Any information that is governed by FERPA [the Family Educational Rights and Privacy Act] is explicitly exempt from the HIPAA rule's definition of protected health information. In general, under FERPA, parents have access to the education records of their unemancipated minor children, including any health information contained in those records. Thus, important questions of interpretation arise when health care is delivered in a school-based health clinic or by a school nurse, or when professionals working in a school have extensive communications about a student's health.

In any specific situation, determining whether the relevant information and records are covered by FERPA or the HIPAA privacy rule requires careful analysis. Most often, however, information that is in the records of a school-based health center, where adolescents often turn with an expectation of confidentiality, is not part of a student's education record. If that is the case, the health center's records would not be subject to FERPA; they would likely be covered by HIPAA. . . .

Constitutional Law Allows Minors to Consent to Family Planning Care

Numerous decisions of the U.S. Supreme Court and other courts recognize that the constitutional right of privacy protects minors as well as adults. These decisions support minors' right to receive contraception without parental consent, even in a state that does not have a law explicitly allowing them to do so. . . .

Dozens of state statutes (most of which are being enforced) require parental consent or notification when a minor seeks an abortion, usually with a "judicial bypass" alternative that allows her to obtain an abortion without parental knowledge or consent. In a state requiring parental consent, if the minor does not use the bypass and allows consent to be obtained from her parents, she will not be considered the individual under the HIPAA rule. If she uses the bypass option, or is in a state that requires parental notification but not consent, the minor will be considered "the individual.". . .

The Records of School-Based Health Centers Must Be Kept Confidential

All school-based health centers require some form of consent from parents before a student who is a minor receives care. Often the parent need only sign a general consent form at the beginning of the school year. Many of these forms specify the services offered at the center, and many specify that services are confidential. However, in general, school-based health centers work hard to involve parents whenever that is possible and appropriate.

Many school-based health centers offer family planning services and STD screening, and often students want and expect that care to be confidential. In every state, minors can legally consent for STD screening; the same is usually true for family planning. As a result, information about STD screening and family planning is in a different category from information about general health care—which the minor may not have the legal right to consent for under state law. Thus, if information about the minor's health and services received at the center is requested either by a parent or by other school personnel, the school-based health center must pay special attention to ensuring that information about family planning and STD screening is not unintentionally disclosed along with other medical records. This is also true if the student's parent has authorized disclosure of health information or medical records to others, such as a new school or a camp. To the extent that confidentiality concerns arise with respect to billing and third-party reimbursement linked to school-based clinics, the same general considerations apply as in a private physician's office. . . .

Finally, school-based health centers may have to address suggestions from school personnel that their records are covered not by HIPAA, but by FERPA. This will rarely be true, as long as school-based health centers or their sponsoring agencies meet the privacy rule's definition of a "covered entity" and center staff are careful to enter protected information only into the health center's record and not into a student's general education records, where it would be accessible to parents under FERPA. Nevertheless, schools and school-based health centers need procedures for determining which records are governed by the requirements of which law and what those requirements mean for how the information can be used with the school. Information about family planning or STD screening in a school-based health center will almost never be accessible to the school, and will be accessible to parents only under specific provisions of state law.

"[School-based health clinics] run roughshod over parental rights by invoking student 'confidentiality.'"

Parents Have the Right to Know When Their Children Receive Family Planning Services at School

Tanya L. Green

Tanya L. Green in the following viewpoint charges that school-based health clinics (SBCs) dispense contraceptives and make abortion referrals without parental consent or knowledge, undermining parental authority. She advocates parental involvement in health care and treatment as being in a child's best interests. By adhering to student confidentiality policies, she contends, most SBCs indirectly encourage a communication gap between parents and their children. Tanya L. Green is special projects writer for Concerned Women for America, a public policy women's organization.

As you read, consider the following questions:
1. According to the viewpoint, what slowed the rapid rise of SBCs and made them nationally known?
2. In Green's contention, how do SBCs circumvent parental authority?
3. What were the immediate and later results of Dorothy Wallis's search for SBCs' violations of parental rights, according to the author?

Tanya L. Green, "Not in My School," *Family Voice*, March/April 2001. Copyright © 2001 by Concerned Women for America. Reproduced by permission.

"The doctor is in." This phrase is taking on a different meaning in schools. Formerly, when a student became ill or injured, the school nurse would administer an aspirin or a Band-Aid. Now, a student needing medical treatment might go to her school's "clinic," where she might also learn about "reproductive health services." An attending staff member might dispense condoms and oral contraceptives, or abortion referrals, without her parents' knowledge or consent.

School-Based Clinics Contribute to the Problem of STDs

The number of school-based clinics (SBCs) rose dramatically over the last decade. According to a 1998-99 survey conducted by the National Assembly on School-Based Health Care (NASBHC), currently 1,135 clinics operate in schools, an increase from only 200 in 1990. Activists had held back SBCs in the 1980s. But the rise of HIV/AIDS played a major role in establishing clinics in the '90s.

"The price was too high in many communities for parents and educators to ignore changing norms," claimed Julia Lear, program director of Making the Grade, a grant program that funds SBCs, in *The Guttmacher Report*. "It became apparent there was a need to bring reproductive health services to high school students."

But the truth is: SBCs don't protect young people from AIDS or other sexually transmitted diseases (STDs).

"The only impact [they have] had is indirectly promoting teens' separation from parents and contributing to the problem . . . of increased STD rates," said Dr. S. DuBose Ravenel, a North Carolina pediatrician and member of the Physician's Resource Council, who has followed data on SBCs for 15 years.

Hidden Motives

School-based clinics often come stealthily, leaving parents unaware until they open. A health department, hospital or private nonprofit organization, which might be pro-abortion, sponsors and organizes the clinics. These outside agencies seek no input from the targeted communities.

Adding "reproductive health services" often comes later, according to *The Guttmacher Report*, a publication related to pro-abortion Planned Parenthood (PP). After the clinics are opened, operators work to build the trust, confidence and familiarity of the community. Then they present "data" on the need of reproductive health services, such as contraceptives.

"As these centers become more established, they gain community support and a buy-in from parents," said John Schlitt, NASBHC's executive director, in *The Guttmacher Report*.

Many clinics also provide pregnancy testing, STD testing and treatment, and HIV testing. Some even provide abortion counseling or referrals. Still others promote the myth of "safer sex" education. Institutions, such as the Robert Wood Johnson Foundation, fund the clinics with no restrictions on "reproductive health" policies.

Sanger's Legacy

SBCs are heavily located exclusively in poor urban, black neighborhoods. This reminds concerned blacks of the 1939 "Negro Project" of Planned Parenthood founder Margaret Sanger.

To hinder black population growth, Sanger opened birth control clinics in poor black neighborhoods. She convinced influential black leaders that birth control was the key to better health for their community. Some in the community saw the truth behind her veiled genocidal scheme, but it still had an impact.

Vestiges of Sanger's plot remain today. As quoted in *USA Today* . . . , the Centers for Disease Control reports the abortion rate in urban areas is higher "where access to abortion is easier." Additionally, 36 percent of all abortions are performed on black women—up from 32 percent in 1990—although blacks constitute 13 percent of the total population.

It should come as no surprise then that PP strongly advocates for SBCs. Its research arm, the Alan Guttmacher Institute, is touted as an "authority" on their benefits and necessity.

The controversy surrounding SBCs in black neighborhoods is not new. In 1986 in Chicago, a group of ministers, parents and students, led by the late Rev. Hiram Crawford, filed a lawsuit against a clinic operating in the all-black Du-

Sable High School. They accused the clinic of "a calculated, pernicious effort to destroy the very fabric of family life among black parents and their children."

Asay. © by Charles Asay. Reproduced by permission.

"If these clinics are so good for black kids, why don't they put them in white areas?" asked Crawford in the November 24, 1986, issue of *Time*. He added that pressure and intimidation by clinic operators initially prevented black parents from challenging school administrators.

Raising Awareness About SBCs' Promotion of Teen Sex

Sadly, the court dismissed the lawsuit, but not without far-reaching effects. "DuSable was the explosion," said Ann Stull, secretary of Illinois' Pro-Life, Pro-Family Coalition. "It slowed down [the rapid growth of] clinics and raised the SBC issue nationally. The process of fighting them became nationally known."

The controversy flared up again in 1998 in Louisiana. Black pro-life state representative Sharon Weston Broome supported SBCs in her Baton Rouge district, if they provided only basic health care for needy students. "Clinics should only promote abstinence," she said.

Broome was appalled when she learned officials planned to place clinics only in black schools, paving the way to add "reproductive health services" down the road. She spoke with Rev. Johnny Hunter, national director of Life Education and Resource Network (LEARN), the largest black pro-life ministry. At his urging, she suggested the clinics be placed in white schools as well. At that suggestion, "the idea was dropped immediately," Hunter reported.

Eugenics and the promotion of teen sexual activity, birth control and abortion constitute reasons enough to reject SBCs—but there's more: insidious undermining of parental authority. Probably because they know parents will not support "reproductive services," SBC operators run roughshod over parental rights by invoking student "confidentiality."

Clinics circumvent parental authority by referring students to an outside agency that provides abortion services or referrals. Some clinics distribute vague forms that simply ask for the parents' "consent" to all services during their child's enrollment period. In many cases, the clinic staff assumes parental consent unless parents say otherwise.

Community Resistance

Chipping away at parental rights causes as much community resistance as the contraceptive/abortion link. When parents realize the clinics' real agenda, they band together to oppose them.

Dorothy Wallis is president and CEO of Caring to Love Ministries, a counseling center for pregnant women in Baton Rouge, Louisiana. She became involved in the school clinic movement in 1986, when private foundations began funding the clinics. The push for contraceptive use concerned her.

"They were only 80-85 percent effective, not 100 percent. There was a false security against pregnancy and STDs. If pregnancy did occur, abortion was a backup," she said. Dorothy also observed the slant toward eugenics: The clinics were being planned only for inner city schools.

In 1996, Gov. Mike Foster appointed her chairman of the School-Based Clinic Task Force, which investigated the clinics. When the Department of Health and Hospitals initially found "no violations" of parental rights, Dorothy waded through "tons and tons of paperwork" on her own. She uncovered vaginal exams, dispensing of contraceptives and "unspoken" abortion referrals—all without parental consent.

As a result, the task force successfully pulled funding from clinics that provided "reproductive health services" and failed to notify parents about services administered to their children. A child must now have prior parental consent before being treated in a school clinic in Louisiana.

But examples from poor, minority neighborhoods do not mean other parents can relax—as developments in an affluent Philadelphia suburb show. In 1999, Linda Pagan contacted Jennifer Siek, chapter coordinator for CWA [Concerned Women for America] of Pennsylvania, for help in defeating clinics planned in her school district. She had learned of the clinics through a friend who was the school's health-care teacher.

Linda put together a phone chain of parents concerned about the birth control, abortion and confidentiality issues. She and Jennifer discussed how to conduct meetings that stressed parental rights.

"We met with [representatives of the hospital involved with the clinic.] . . . [They] did not like the questions we had, and to this day have not answered them," Linda says. "Eventually, the offer to staff and run health clinics in our schools was dropped. The school district was taking on the responsibility of the parent. That is not in the best interest of the child."

Parental Ignorance Is Bliss

All parents, regardless of race or socioeconomic status, must diligently protect their children's health and their parental rights. Barbara Thomas, executive director of Louisiana's North Baton Rouge Women's Help Center, said parents are key, but added that many parents in her district are passing their responsibility onto teachers and pastors.

"Half the battle is getting through pastors," Barbara says. "A lot of African-American pastors have a bit more liberal theology when it comes to abortion. I have attended health fairs at various black churches in my community and witnessed people dispensing condoms to teens."

To combat this, Barbara educates pastors about the harmful effects of teen sexual activity and abortion on the community—and that SBCs aren't the answer.

Many family structures, particularly in urban areas, are weakened by the absence of a father. Therefore, ministries must meet their special needs. The undermining of parental rights by SBCs only further weakens an already fragile structure.

SBC promoters effectively strategize to put contraceptives, abortion referrals and other reproductive health services into the schools. For them, parental ignorance is bliss.

Parents must therefore stay informed of developments at their children's schools. They must make their voices heard when administrators attempt to usurp their authority by making decisions for their children.

> *"It is problematic when the government examines our educational records because [it] invites suspicion based on the things we study, read and discuss."*

The Patriot Act Threatens Students' Privacy Rights

Amy Miller and Ryan Lozar

Amy Miller and Ryan Lozar argue in the following viewpoint that provisions of the Patriot Act that grant the government access to students' school and library records have a chilling effect on educational freedom. Before the Patriot Act, laws protected students' right to privacy and required probable cause before records could be reviewed, they maintain, but now privacy can be violated if there is only suspicion of a crime. Worse, they claim, students are not informed when their records are released, removing public scrutiny from the equation. Amy Miller and Ryan Lozar are law clerks who wrote this for the American Civil Liberties Union of Ohio.

As you read, consider the following questions:

1. According to the authors, what ultimately results from the "loss of transparency" under the Patriot Act?
2. Before the Patriot Act, what two protections do the authors say that FERPA offered to students in regard to their educational records?
3. What is the difference between probable cause and reasonable suspicion, according to Miller and Lozar?

Amy Miller and Ryan Lozar, "Impact of the USA Patriot Act on FERPA," www.acluohio.org, August 2002. Copyright © 2002 by the American Civil Liberties Union of Ohio. Reproduced by permission.

Anti-terrorism legislation passed since the September 11th attacks on New York City, Washington, D.C., and Pennsylvania has far-reaching tentacles that limit student privacy in educational institutions in this country. Whereas the Family Educational Rights and Privacy Act of 1974 (FERPA) sought to guarantee students in the United States privacy rights, the "Uniting and Strengthening America by Providing Appropriate Tools Required to Intercept and Obstruct Terrorism Act of 2001" (USA PATRIOT Act) undermines student privacy by cutting swaths of exceptions out of FERPA. The recent reduction of student privacy rights created by the USA PATRIOT Act allows law enforcement officials to throw out a large net requesting student information without probable cause of wrongdoing by the students covered by their search. Students' private education records will be under greater law enforcement scrutiny than in previous years.

The USA PATRIOT Act Has a Chilling Effect

Why should we care if the government examines our education records, anyway? It is problematic when the government examines our education records because aggregation of such personal information invites suspicion based on the things we study, read and discuss. The USA PATRIOT Act's loosening of educational privacy may make students think twice about engaging in educational pursuits that have to do with politically volatile topics. Not only is educational freedom for the sake of educational freedom impacted, but another result is a dearth of viewpoint diversity which is necessary for well-balanced social and political debate. Students and teachers must have the freedom to offer and take courses, give lectures or choose paper topics, and read about any subject of interest without fear of government suspicion, persecution, and reprisal.

Imagine law enforcement red-flagging your name because they noticed you took a course in Islamic law, went to a meeting for the Arab-American Anti-Defamation League, or tutored Muslim students. These innocent actions could make you subject to further governmental investigation. The loss of transparency under the USA PATRIOT Act compounds the chilling effect on educational freedom because not only can the government look at your education records more easily, but you never know *when* they will exercise that right to increased access. The result is that students will simply have to remain politically correct 100% of the time in the courses they take, the lectures they attend, and people they sit with in the cafeteria, lest Uncle Sam be watching.

When we step with such care, the value of education and free thought is lost. The government has already decided our political and social norms, and we must comply with them or be suspect, dissension be damned.

How FERPA's Tough Standards Protected Privacy

The Family Educational Rights and Privacy Act of 1974 (FERPA) is a provision of the Education Amendments of 1974 guaranteeing parents and students the right to privacy with regard to all material in their educational record. When the law was passed, Congress saw the value of FERPA as protecting students' right to privacy by limiting the transferability of their education records without consent.

FERPA applies to all educational institutions that receive funds from any applicable program of the United States Department of Education. This department's law enforcement arm, the Family Policy Compliance Office, has the ability to cut off federal funding to any educational institution that is violating FERPA provisions. Generally, FERPA bars any educational institution receiving federal funds from releasing a student's educational record without his/her permission, or parental permission if the student is younger than eighteen years of age.

FERPA [before the September 11, 2001, terrorist attacks] bore few exceptions to the prohibition of the release of students' education records to third parties. Most significant among these exceptions was the ability to circumvent student consent by obtaining a subpoena or court order to achieve access to education records.

But the use of this exception was tempered by two requirements: 1) a subpoena or court order could only be issued upon cause, and 2) the release of education records pursuant to a subpoena or court order was disclosed to the

Under the Patriot Act, the Government Can Access a Broad Range of Private Records

Americans do not agree that the [Patriot] Act will do what its supporters purportedly claim. It was passed in the heat of the moment without adequate congressional review and debate, and without regard to the harm it does to the constitutional liberties that define us as a nation. As currently constituted, it lets the government find out what a person has been reading in a public library, what they keep on their home computer or in their office financial records. The targeted person does not have to be informed of the searches before or, in some cases, afterward. Nor does the targeted person have to be a terrorism suspect.

The Patriot Act should be viewed as a metaphor for all the civil liberties violations that are currently occurring. . . . Section 215 gives the government the power to get records from any business, permits federal investigators to seize library, financial, health, education and other personal records from cities, all without showing that the suspect is a terrorist, a criminal, or even a foreign agent. . . . No probable cause need be shown, and there are criminal penalties for disclosing that records have been requested. It also compels Internet service providers to turn over information about their customers or subscribers in counterterrorism or counterintelligence cases WITHOUT a judge's approval. . . .

Apparently . . . American citizens have no rights that prosecutors or investigators need respect, especially if they claim the magic words, "war on terror." But you don't have to be a terrorist or suspected of terrorist activities. The law was written to apply to all crimes, not just those related to terrorism. As a result, we are closer to a totalitarian state than ever before in our history.

Joe Williams, interviewed by Jamie Glazov, FrontPageMagazine.com, May 18, 2004.

---

student whose record was released.

Requiring cause before the issuance of a subpoena or court order was no small hurdle. Even more importantly, though, the disclosure requirement opened up the entire process to public scrutiny. Public accountability is important because it curbs the abuse of individual rights by government actors.

All in all, pre-September 11 FERPA recognized both the needs of law enforcement officials and the privacy rights of individuals, and tried to strike a balance between the two and respect the importance of each.

The USA PATRIOT Act Lowers Standards

The "Uniting and Strengthening America by Providing Appropriate Tools Required to Intercept and Obstruct Terrorism Act of 2001" is a 342 page, quickly-passed law that imposes extra burdens on all Americans who participate in quite innocent activities or organizations that happen to be blacklisted as terrorist organizations. The terrorism-fighting tools of the title have a primary purpose of making it more expedient for law enforcement to investigate suspected terrorists.

The USA PATRIOT Act, as it relates to FERPA, creates a special set of compliance rules for the Attorney General or any federal officer in a position not lower than an assistant attorney general. These law enforcement officials are given the power to receive a special court order permitting access to a student's education records provided there are facts giving rise to believe the information is needed for an authorized investigation. This easier search method encompasses lower standards to gain access to student education records.

The USA PATRIOT Act alters educational privacy in many respects, but the two most egregious alterations are:

• the new law subjects students' private education records to a lower threshold of review than the traditional probable cause, and

• it eliminates the necessary transparency by not requiring an educational institution to inform the student that his files have been released.

First, the language of the USA PATRIOT Act states that judicial issuance of a court order granting access to a student's education records can occur at the existence of *specific and articulable facts*, giving reason to believe that the education records are likely to be relevant to an authorized investigation by the Attorney General of an act of domestic or international terrorism. Requiring "specific and articulable facts" for issuance of the court order subjects the privacy invasion to a reasonable suspicion standard, a much lower standard than the probable cause standard. Where probable cause requires law enforcement officials to know what they are looking for before they look for it, reasonable suspicion does not. As a result, using reasonable suspicion has traditionally been used as justification for only minor privacy invasions, such as when police officers pat down an individual exhibiting unusual or suspicious behavior. Poring over a student's education records is not such a minor intrusion.

Eliminating Transparency Is Harmful

A second problematic aspect to the USA PATRIOT Act is that it eliminates the transparency that was an obligatory part of all releases of education records under pre-September 11 FERPA. As mentioned earlier, FERPA required that every educational institution maintain records as to whom students' education records were released. With the USA PATRIOT Act's new amendment to FERPA, educational institutions are not required to inform the student of the release of their education records to the law enforcement officials enumerated therein. In fact, educational institutions are granted immunity by the USA PATRIOT Act from loss of federal funding for releasing any information without a student's consent, so long as they are releasing records pursuant to the USA PATRIOT Act in good faith. The difficulty here is that the educational institution could be releasing your education records left and right to the government and you would not even know it.

Transparency in government actions, such as the requisitioning of education records, as here, is important because public scrutiny is an integral tool in the avoidance of governmental abuse of power and shows respect for individual rights. We can only challenge the government's unjustified violation of our individual rights when we know those rights are violated.

"National Security is one thing, but aggressive policies that invade the privacy of students who just want to learn and voice their opinions is another."

The Patriot Act Infringes on International Students' Privacy Rights

Part I: Sonia Mukhi; Part II: Kate McCormack

The authors of the following two-part viewpoint maintain that the Patriot Act permits the government to monitor international students without cause, violating their privacy rights. In Part I, Sonia Mukhi, a student in the School of Foreign Service at Georgetown University, declares that the Patriot Act is racist because it allows campus police and the FBI to report on the activities of students of Middle Eastern background. In Part II, Kate McCormack decries the act's national monitoring system for nonresident students. She claims that harsh punishments are issued for minor visa violations. McCormack is a senior in international studies and psychology at the University of Wisconsin–Madison.

As you read, consider the following questions:

1. What right does Mukhi say DPS has now?
2. For what reasons might an international student be deported under SEVIS, according to McCormack?
3. In McCormack's contention, what threatening option does the Patriot Act leave open?

Part I: Sonia Mukhi, "USA Patriot Act Violates Civil Liberties of Students," *The Hoya*, April 15, 2003. Copyright © 2003 by *The Hoya*. All rights reserved. Reproduced by permission. Part II: Kate McCormack, "SEVIS Violates Our International Students' Civil Liberties," *Daily Cardinal*, February 23, 2004. Copyright © 2004 by the Daily Cardinal Media Corporation. Reproduced by permission.

I

The university, the academic institution, is traditionally the breeding ground of discovery and knowledge. This premise functions on the fact that we, as affiliates of an educational establishment, have the freedom to investigate, learn and speak up about the knowledge we gain. If this is taken away from us, we have nothing.

Enough of the flowery introduction as to why I think civil liberties are good and are necessary on college campuses. The plain issue that I wish to address is Georgetown University's (along with many other schools in the U.S.) compliance with the FBI in screening and tracking down "suspicious" students on college campuses. To be less vague, and in turn less politically correct—"suspicious" students often being international students of Middle Eastern/Arab/Muslim background.

Campus Police as Spies

Apparently, as indicated in the Patriot Act, campus police are able and willing to be used as localized monitors overseen by the federal government. To specify the issue to our particular Georgetown situation, DPS [Department of Public Safety] has the right to find out what books we check out of the library, find out what kinds of political convictions we express in our classes and around campus and go to other ridiculous lengths to screen our daily activities.

I think Younus Mirza ([Georgetown University School of Foreign Service] '04), who is a part of Campaign Civil Rights, has said it correctly: "Campus police are supposed to provide security for students, but if they are spying on us that provides a certain sense of insecurity." No one opposed to this new legislation is in the dark about the fact that at least two of the hijackers of [the September 11, 2001, terrorist attacks] came to the United States on student visas and that this is a big concern for all Americans. But, what I think needs to be understood, are the implications that all of this has in the long run. History is cyclic—this isn't the first time wartime policies limiting civil liberties have reached the University. The CIA and FBI have notoriously investigated on campuses during the Cold War/Vietnam era. Plenty of books have been written on the issue and it is definitely not a crazy conspiracy theory, but a rather harsh reality of our nation's history.

It's happening again, and the issue is as controversial and dangerous as it ever was.

But why should we care, right? We shouldn't have anything to hide. It's a really logical and sound question to ask yourself if your hands are clean and you are just a Joe/Jane . . . going about your college education. However it's also an incredibly easy question to ask yourself when you know you aren't the ones they are watching.

The Patriot Act Is Racist

National Security is one thing, but aggressive policies that invade the privacy of students who just want to learn and voice their opinions is another. I think it's rather naive to assume, especially in this day and age, that America lives up to the ideals of liberty and freedom as exerted in the constitution. The Patriot Acts are blatant evidence that the U.S. Constitution has taken a back seat to the current administration's desire to accumulate power on the premise of "wartime necessity" and exert its racist and imposing doctrine. The implication of these government-sponsored violations is, however, a different story for a different day.

Amid this background is the most urgent issue, which is that of these violations reaching Georgetown, our home, where we should have the freedom to think and feel as we do. Even if it doesn't affect you personally, it affects your community. It affects many of the people who you know should not be perceived as a threat, but are antagonized for their beliefs—or even their ethnic background. Many of these "suspects" are peaceful international students who have already mustered up the courage to leave their respective countries and come here to receive one of the best educations in the world. What kind of an education can they gain if they are afraid what their knowledge will do to them? Unfortunately, there's not much we concerned citizens can do to protect our freedoms given the current political climate.

As students, however, we are certainly empowered—and

The Monitoring of International Students Raises Privacy Concerns

Ahmed Makani was busy this summer [2002] looking up classes and anticipating his next four years at Yale—that is, until the U.S. embassy in his native Pakistan informed him that he would not be allowed to enter America in the fall. According to Makani, the embassy informed him that the student visa necessary for him to travel to the U.S. had been placed on "indefinite hold" without any further explanation. "There are many other students [with] placements in very good universities who are facing the same situation," Makani said. . . .

The unexpected difficulties that . . . Makani [has] experienced are just the first fallout from a larger movement begun by the Oct. 2001 passage of the USA PATRIOT Act, which [stipulates the formation of a national monitoring system] known as Sevis—the Student and Exchange Visitor Information System. . . .

Despite the difficulties of implementation and possible infringements of information privacy raised by Sevis, even civil liberties and international student watchdog groups seem to be offering the new program tentative approval. . . .

[Have the September 11, 2001, terrorist attacks] changed Americans' view of the value of personal information privacy? While some have already begun to speak ominously of a developing "surveillance society," most . . . seem willing to sacrifice the personal information privacy of international visitors for the sake of some broader sense of security. Such a revision of values worries Chris Hoofnagle, Legislative Counsel at the Electronic Privacy Information Center (EPIC), a think tank in Washington, D.C. Hoofnagle warns of the "risk that people lose sight of the value of civil liberties for perhaps the illusion of security."

Justin Chen, *Yale Herald*, September 6, 2002.

---

we have the muscle to affect policies on our campus. I hope to see an end to these rampant infringements of our right to live freely and an increased empathy and understanding of the plight of those who will really be affected by these wartime policies.

II

Imagine having to notify the government any time you wanted to change your major, drop a class or go home for a break. It sounds ludicrous and restrictive but as a result of new federal legislation invasion of privacy, bureaucratic hoop-jumping and an increasing threat of arbitrary deportation have become a reality for the international student community both here at UW [University of Wisconsin]-Madison and throughout the nation.

SEVIS, the Student and Exchange Visitor Information System, is a national Internet-based monitoring system for all non-resident students studying in the United States. SEVIS is run by the Immigration and Naturalization Services, but it essentially allows a wide variety of government offices to use institutions of learning to gain access to student information. SEVIS was forced through as part of the USA Patriot Act and came into effect in January 2003. It not only increases the amount of people who have access to student information but substantially increases the amount of required information calling for an extensive background check, and what is more ominous, anything else deemed "relevant" by the government such as personal "books, records, papers, documents and other items."

Privacy Violations and Harsh Punishments

SEVIS is disturbing on a variety of levels. On an individual level, it strips previous legislation, mainly the Family Education Records Protection Act designed to protect privacy and imposes inappropriately harsh punishments (mainly deportation) for small errors. On a technical level, it is full of systematic errors, which cause extremely long delays in visa processing and can lead to inappropriate deportation. Finally, it is symbolic of a wave of legislation that creates an intimidating and hostile atmosphere . . . and violates the civil liberties and freedoms of all U.S. residents.

Under SEVIS, students can be deported for the following reasons: failure to report an address change to the INS [Immigration and Naturalization Service] within 10 days, dropping below a full-time credit load without prior permission or an unauthorized major change. Even when students follow the rules to the letter they can still get into trouble due to SEVIS's extremely slow processing of information. For example a student could apply for a visa at the proper time but due to delays, their current visa could run out while they are waiting—leaving them subject to deportation! Additionally, if students leave the United States to visit home for a break or for a family emergency they can subsequently be denied re-entry to the country—and thus the ability to finish their degrees.

SEVIS is a mandatory program but receives minimal federal funding and therefore has led to the absurd conclusion of international students paying for their own "monitoring." Currently a UW-Madison task force is investigating more equitable ways to pay for the system. Across the country, however, a majority of international students have been unjustly charged a fee for a program that is supposedly intended to be for "the good and security" of all U.S. citizens.

SEVIS Threatens the Rights of International Students

Technical errors and privacy invasion are not even the most important issues at stake—international students can also be sanctioned or deported for "misconduct," a term broad enough to include political activity or even the protesting of SEVIS itself. These loopholes within the system are fundamental violations of freedom of speech and assembly and can act as an informal form of "silencing" the international student body—a dynamic group who bring alternative visions to campuses and the country.

SEVIS is only one part of the more comprehensive and the more invasive USA Patriot Act. The Patriot Act extends police surveillance powers, expands the definition of terrorism to include domestic political groups, allows citizens to be investigated without probable cause if it is for "intelligence purposes" and permits non-citizen suspects convicted of no crime to be detained indefinitely without judicial review. The Patriot Act also leaves the option for a SEVIS like monitoring system to be expanded to any student, citizen or not, involved in political activity which the government deems "threatening." This type of legislation threatens our ability to work for change within society and acts to silence voices of dissent.

*"The fundamental question facing
Americans today is not the false trade-off
between security and liberty, but rather
how we can use security to protect liberty."*

The Patriot Act Protects Privacy Rights

Part I: Viet D. Dinh; Part II: Johnny N. Williams

The authors of the following two-part viewpoint contend that
the Patriot Act protects privacy rights while helping law enforcement fight terrorism. In Part I, Viet D. Dinh, former assistant attorney general for the Office of Legal Policy who
oversaw the drafting and implementation of the Patriot Act,
claims that fears that the act violates privacy are unfounded.
The act constrains the government's powers to access records,
he assures Americans. In Part II, Johnny N. Williams, in a
speech to the U.S. House of Representatives, maintains that
the Patriot Act's monitoring system for international students
combats fraud and enhances national security without infringing on students' privacy rights. Williams is interim director
for Immigration Interior Enforcement.

As you read, consider the following questions:

1. In Dinh's contention, how does the Patriot Act protect
   Americans' free speech rights?
2. According to Williams, how does ICE prioritize student
   violators?

Part I: Viet D. Dinh, "How the USA Patriot Act Defends Democracy," www.
freerepublic.com, June 1, 2004. Copyright © 2004 by The Foundation for the
Defense of Democracies. Reproduced by permission. Part II: Johnny N.
Williams, statement before the U.S. House of Representatives Subcommittee on
Immigration, Border Security and Claims, Committee on the Judiciary,
Washington, DC, April 2, 2003.

I

Passed soon after the terrorist attacks of [September 11, 2001], the USA Patriot Act is one of the most important legislative measures in American history. The Act enables the government to fight what will undoubtedly be a long and difficult war against international terrorism. At the same time, the Act constrains the government, preventing any government attempt to unjustifiably extend its powers.

Yet the Patriot Act, despite its near-unanimous passage through Congress, has also become one of the most vilified pieces of legislation in living memory. Critics charge that the Act allows for extensive domestic surveillance of US citizens engaged in peaceful, law-abiding activities, that the Act could potentially turn the US into a police state. While some of the rhetoric deployed against the Patriot Act is hyperbolic, the concerns expressed about official surveillance of US citizens are reasonable and should be addressed. The vehemence of many of those who oppose the Patriot Act is a reflection of their attachment to our Constitution, even if, as this paper will argue, many of their fears about government surveillance are unfounded.

Using Security to Protect Liberty

Rather than reply to the crescendo of complaints and exaggerated claims in kind, what is needed is a constructive conversation about security and liberty, about the success of our terrorism prevention efforts and the need to protect and defend American freedom. We need to assess the experience of past years to ensure both that officials have the tools necessary to protect us and that there are safeguards to check against misuse of those tools. The national debate will be constructive if we can lower the heat and turn up the light.

The fundamental question facing Americans today is not the false trade-off between security and liberty, but rather how we can use security to protect liberty. Any debate over security and liberty must start with the recognition that the primary threat to American freedom comes from al-Qaeda and other [terrorist] groups that seek to kill Americans, not from the men and women of law enforcement agencies who protect them from that danger. That the American homeland has not suffered another terrorist attack since September 11, 2001, is a testament to the remarkable efforts of law enforcement, intelligence, and homeland security personnel. Their hard work, dedication and increased coordination have been greatly aided by the tools, resources and guidance that Congress provided in the Patriot Act. . . .

Fears About the Patriot Act Are Unfounded

Shouting voices are ignoring questions that are critical to both security and liberty. Lost among the understandable fears about what the government could be doing are the facts about what the government actually is doing. Overheated rhetoric over minor legal alterations has overshadowed profoundly important questions about fundamental changes in law and policy.

There has been widespread condemnation of Section 215 of the Patriot Act, the so-called "library records" provision. The debate over Section 215 illustrates how awry the direction of the debate has gone. Critics have railed against the provision as allowing a return to J. Edgar Hoover's monitoring of private citizens' reading habits. The American Civil Liberties Union (ACLU) has sued the government, claiming that the provision, through its mere existence, foments a chilling fear among Muslim organizations and activists. Others, more fancifully, have claimed that Section 215 allows the government to act as Big Brother, snooping on innocent citizens in a manner reminiscent of George Orwell's *1984*.

These fears are sincere. They are also historically and legally unfounded. Not only does the Patriot Act end the anomaly that allows such records to be routinely seen by investigators in criminal cases while preventing their access by counter-terrorism officials, the legislation provides more protections than usually occurs when records are subject to subpoena. For years, Grand Juries have issued subpoenas to businesses to hand over records relevant to criminal inquiries. Section 215 of the Patriot Act gives courts, for national security investigations, the same power to issue similar orders to businesses, from chemical makers to explosives dealers. Section 215 is not aimed at bookstores or libraries.

Like its criminal grand jury equivalent, Section 215 orders are written with business records in mind but could, if necessary, be applied to reading materials acquired by a terrorist suspect.

Protections for Average Americans and Criminals

Contrary to what the critics claim, Section 215 is narrow in scope. The FBI cannot use Section 215 to investigate garden-variety crimes, nor even domestic terrorism. Instead, Section 215 can be used only to "obtain foreign intelligence information not concerning a United States person," or to "protect against international terrorism or clandestine intelligence activities." The records of average Americans, and even not-so-average criminals, are simply beyond the reach of Section 215.

The fact that Section 215 applies uniquely to national security investigations means that the orders are confidential. As such secrecy raises legitimate concerns, Congress embedded significant checks into the issuing of Section 215 warrants. First, a federal judge alone can issue and supervise a Section 215 order. By contrast, Grand Jury subpoenas for records are routinely issued by the court clerk. Second, the government must report to Congress every six months the number of times, and the manner, of the provision's use. On October 17, 2002, the House Judiciary Committee stated that its review of the information "has not given rise to any concern that the authority is being misused or abused." Moreover, in September 2003, the Attorney General made public the previously classified information that Section 215 had not been used once since its passage.

The Patriot Act Preserves Civil Liberties

It may well be that the clamor over Section 215 reflects a different concern, closely related to the cherished American tradition of free speech. Some seem to fear the government can use ordinary criminal investigative tools to easily obtain records from purveyors of First Amendment activities, such as libraries and bookstores. Again the fundamental concern is as understandable as the specific fear related to Section 215 is unjustified. The prohibition in Section 215 that investigations "not be conducted of a United States person solely

152

upon the basis of activities protected by the first amendment of the Constitution of the United States" addresses this problem directly and makes the Patriot Act more protective of civil liberties than ordinary criminal procedure. . . .

The Government Is Unconcerned with the Activities of Innocent Americans

With an election year on the horizon, and opportunists cynically turning "Patriot" into a codeword for oppressive overreach, it has become critically important to raise public awareness about what the Patriot Act is and why its provisions are so necessary—indeed, were such a no-brainer that they sailed through Congress with overwhelming bipartisan support. . . .

Manipulating public opinion, [opponents] spread the fallacy that our fundamental rights are under assault—a fallacy that is fast becoming popular wisdom. . . .

The government rarely, if ever, has need to invade the privacy of Americans' viewing habits—indeed, even his ardent detractors haven't yet wasted much energy on the image of [Attorney General John] Ashcroft fretting that someone, somewhere may be watching *Sex and the City* (although they have notoriously slandered him for purportedly using the Patriot Act to ponder our library checkouts). . . .

Of all the *argumentum ad hominem* aimed at Ashcroft, this is the most inane. The bookshelves of thoughtful people run the gamut from Dickens to Disney and most anything in between; seeing their library checkouts would tell us precious little about their propensity, if any, toward crime. After two decades in law enforcement, I can now break the secret: The government doesn't care what you read (a fact that would be palpable to anyone who'd slogged through a Justice Department press release). Consequently, it should shock no one that, as the beleaguered Ashcroft recently reported, the government has not yet sought library records a single time under the Patriot Act.

Andrew C. McCarthy, *National Review Online*, November 13, 2003.

The Patriot Act's surveillance provisions are not the executive grab for power and extension of government that many portray them to be. Rather the Act sensibly updates the law to keep pace with changing technology, tidies up confused legal interpretations and standardizes powers while restraining them. The Act gives the government the tools it needs to fight terrorism while observing the cherished liberties of Americans. Counterterrorism is a dynamic process, and the Patriot Act is not written in stone. It will be scrutinized by the courts, debated by the citizenry and amended by Congress.

We have to recognize that our nation is navigating uncharted waters. We have been forced to fight an unprovoked conflict, a war declared against us by nihilistic terrorists, not by our traditional adversary, a nation-state. During these times, when the foundation of liberty is under attack, it is critical that we both reaffirm the ideals of our constitutional democracy and also discern the techniques necessary to secure those ideals against the threat of terrorism. As Karl Llewellyn, the renowned law professor, once observed: "Ideals without technique are a mess. But technique without ideals is a menace." The Patriot Act, by combining ideals and technique, is the domestic shield of American democracy, a protection deserving of renewal by our Congress.

II

Thank you for the opportunity to update the [House of Representatives] on the deployment of the Bureau of Immigration and Customs Enforcement's (ICE) Student and Exchange Visitor Information System (SEVIS)—a new Internet-based system that greatly enhances the government's ability to manage and monitor foreign students and exchange program visitors and their dependents during their stay in the United States.[1] SEVIS maintains critical, up-to-date information that can be accessed electronically, making it a powerful tool for combating fraud and for ensuring that individuals comply with the terms of their visa, activities that are vital to enhancing homeland security.

The Purpose of SEVIS

State Department consular officers overseas now have instant access to this information, improving their ability to decide whether to issue a student visa. This information is also available to the Bureau of Customs and Border Protection (BCBP) officers at ports-of-entry (POEs), allowing them to better

---

1. SEVIS was implemented as part of the 2001 Patriot Act.

track the entry of students and exchange visitors and to guarantee that the visa holder is the same person to whom it was issued. Additionally, personnel at Bureau of Citizenship and Immigration Services (BCIS) Service Centers are using this information to better adjudicate applications for benefits.

SEVIS was initially a project of the Immigration and Naturalization Service (INS), where it was developed and deployed by the Immigration Services Division (now BCIS). When INS transitioned into the Department of Homeland Security (DHS) on March 1 [2003], responsibility for SEVIS shifted to ICE, as mandated by the Homeland Security Act. The two bureaus are working hand-in-hand to assure a smooth transition of the system.

The system is part of the overall Student and Exchange Visitor Program (SEVP), the other functions of which include certifying schools for accepting foreign students, internal and external training, fee collection, and enforcement. SEVIS tracks information about an individual's school admission, visa issuance, entry into the United States, registration for classes, changes of address, program of study, program extensions, and employment authorization. It enables schools and exchange program sponsors to quickly update information they are required to send to the DHS and the Department of State (DOS) throughout the duration of a student or exchange visitor's stay in the United States. . . .

Since implementation, SEVIS has performed very effectively, but it has not been without issues. Most problems are quickly addressed and resolved. For example, the intermittent inability of some schools to access the system and users timing out before they could complete their desired task had occurred. In early March [2003], the system was taken off line for 15 minutes and the necessary fixes were made to remedy these performance problems. Currently, the only outstanding issue has to do with an issue known as "bleeding," the unintended merging of data from one school to another which results in the printing of legitimate student information at the wrong institution. ICE has hired an additional contractor specifically to address this issue, which is an issue of privacy, not accuracy. The information in SEVIS is the important component of the system and how that information enhances our ability to track foreign students. Bleeding does not affect the accuracy of the foreign student information. . . .

SEVIS Allows the Government to Track Student Violators

SEVIS is updated at the time of an individual student's entry to the United States. The Enhanced Border Security and Visa Entry Reform Act (Border Security Act) of 2002 requires schools to report foreign students who fail to enroll within 30 days of the schools' registration deadline. Schools appoint foreign student advisors who are required to maintain foreign student information and assist the students and the school in adhering to the laws and regulations of the Immigration and Nationality Act. These advisors, known as designated school officials, are responsible for reporting student "no shows" to the ICE Immigration Investigation Program Headquarters either by calling a dedicated toll-free number or by electronically "flagging" the student's record in SEVIS as a "no show." More than 1,800 "no show" students have been reported to ICE through the toll-free number.

After a "no show" has been reported, ICE has the Law Enforcement Support Center run database checks. All referrals confirmed to have entered the United States, and for which no record of departure exists, are subject to further indices searches. Student status violators who may present a heightened security risk are immediately referred to the ICE National Security Unit for appropriate action. All others are being prioritized based upon other factors such as criminal history and prior adverse immigration history, and then referred to the appropriate field office. All student violators are entered into the National Automated Immigration Lookout System to ensure replacement visas are not inadvertently issued, and to ensure any subsequent attempts to enter the United States are scrutinized. ICE is committed to enforcing our immigration laws against violators identified through SEVIS. This is founded in our belief that effective compliance enforcement against student violators is a critical component of the SEVIS system.

There has been some concern in the school community that SEVIS errors have been responsible for unwarranted enforcement actions being taken against students. ICE can assure the public that it does not rely solely on information in SEVIS. Prior to taking an enforcement action, ICE agents review each individual case, including interviewing potential violators, to confirm that action is warranted. ICE will only take action against immigration law violators when action is warranted.

SEVIS is part of the Homeland Security mosaic. It is deployed now and in the next year it will develop and grow as a program, increasing its ability to manage and monitor foreign students and exchange visitors in order to ensure that they arrive in the United States, register at the school or exchange visitor program, and maintain their status during their stay as valued guests in this country. SEVIS enhances our ability to detect and deter those who may come to America for nefarious purposes, while extending a hand in friendship to those seeking the exceptional education and training opportunities this great country has to offer. SEVIS allows our nation to strike the proper balance between openness to international students and exchange visitors and the necessary security obtained by enforcing our nation's laws.

Periodical Bibliography

The following articles have been selected to supplement the diverse views presented in this chapter.

Advocates for Youth	"Legal Issues and School-Based and School-Linked Health Centers," June 1998. www.advocatesforyouth.org.
Justin Chen	"Under Scrutiny: Privacy on Campus," *Yale Herald*, September 6, 2002.
Charlie Crist	"Florida School Search Manual: Legal Guidelines for Student Searches at Public Schools," 2004. http://myfloridalegal.com.
Kathy Davis et al.	"Surveillance in Schools: Safety vs. Personal Privacy," University of Illinois at Urbana-Champaign. http://students.ed.uiuc.edu/jkelsey/surveillance.
Electronic Frontier Foundation	"Let the Sun Set on PATRIOT—Section 215: 'Access to Records and Other Items Under the Foreign Intelligence Surveillance Act,'" February 18, 2004. www.eff.org.
Jeff Jacoby	"Overblown Fears About the Patriot Act," May 24, 2004. www.townhall.com.
Renee Jenkins	"Protecting the Rights of Conscience of Health Care Providers and a Parent's Right to Know," American Academy of Pediatrics, July 11, 2002. www.aap.org.
Jack Keller	"School Searches," New York State Police, School & Community Outreach Unit, May 20, 2003. www.cnypolice.com.
National Family Planning & Reproductive Health Association	"Mandatory Parental Involvement for Reproductive Health Services," March 31, 2004. www.nfprha.org.
Office of the Vice President for Research at Virginia Tech	"Anti-Terrorism Laws," June 9, 2003. www.research.vt.edu.
Troy Pickard	"Patriot Act a Threat to Our Library Usage," *Panther*, Chapman University, May 12, 2003.
Arlon Staywell	"Bill Would Notify Parents When Kids Get Help for Drugs or STDs," Capital News Service, February 8, 2003.
Washington Times	"Hype, Hysteria, and the Patriot Act," August 26, 2003.

CHAPTER 4

Do School Drug Policies Violate Students' Rights?

Chapter Preface

A 2001 survey revealed that at least 46 percent of tenth graders have tried an illegal drug, and 23 percent of students in that grade had used in the past month. While drug abuse by anyone is a concern, the Office of National Drug Control Policy (ONDCP) points out that youths' immature physical and psychological development makes them more susceptible than adults to drugs' harmful effects. Besides impacting the lives of users and their families, drug use in schools has a great economic impact. Estimates by the ONDCP indicate that substance abuse added at least $41 billion to the costs of elementary and secondary education for the 2000–2001 school year.

In an effort to combat student drug use, schools have implemented controversial policies such as random drug testing to detect and discipline student drug users. In light of statistics showing that treatment is an effective solution, some schools give drug offenders the option of undergoing treatment rather than being suspended or expelled, the most common sanctions for student drug use. As lawyer Barton Aronson contends, we should "give them treatment, counseling, and attention. . . . We should never write off children as criminals until we've tried to help. . . . Trying to correct kids rather than punish them is what grownups are supposed to do." However, drug treatment is contentious. At issue is whether mandatory drug treatment programs are effective and whether they violate students' rights.

Many people believe mandatory treatment works. Editorial writer Marjorie Cortez maintains that the sooner drug abuse is detected, the more effective interventions can be. She writes, "There's obviously a benefit to ferreting out drug use at its early stages when treatment and other interventions can be highly successful." However, others disagree, claiming mandatory treatment is unsuccessful and unlikely to benefit youth who do not wish to stop using chemicals. Furthermore, Baldwin Research, which develops recovery programs for chemical abusers, asserts that most treatment programs have not been proven to be effective and do not produce long-term results, especially in adolescents. Baldwin claims, "Studies of conventional treatment of adolescents yielded a 0%

success rate over a 14 month period post treatment."

Another controversial element of mandatory drug treatment programs is whether they infringe on students' rights. Many critics contend that schools use too wide a net when determining which students should be required to undergo treatment. Joel Brown of the Center for Educational Research and Development estimates that less than 10 percent of students required to undergo treatment have a drug problem. Youth who do not use drugs regularly and who always use in moderation, he explains, will not benefit from treatment. Journalist Jake Ginsky calls this level of drug use "by most people's standards, nothing remarkable for an American adolescent, certainly no worse than that of hundreds of other healthy, thriving teenagers." Yet many of those students are labeled addicts, Brown says, and they and their parents are forced into expensive long-term programs. Libertarians feel that even though mandatory treatment policies are designed to help youth, they violate privacy and undermine trust. Opponents of these policies question whether schools, in an attempt to maintain a safe, drug-free environment, are justified in infringing on students' rights.

Many commentators, however, maintain that violating students' rights in order to treat those who need help recovering from drug abuse is an appropriate trade-off. If requiring thousands of youth to attend treatment helps just one child, it would be worthwhile, they say. Aronson asks, "If sending kids to drug treatment is the right thing to do, are we being overly concerned with their right to privacy . . . if the only result of violating it is to provide [them] with a benefit [they] so desperately need?"

Mandatory drug treatment programs for students remains controversial. The authors in this chapter struggle with the issue of how to balance students' constitutional rights with their right to attend a drug-free school. As mandatory treatment makes clear, maintaining a positive balance between these competing interests is difficult.

"Students are assumed guilty until they can produce a clean urine sample, with little regard given to students' privacy rights."

Random Drug Testing Is Harmful and Infringes on Students' Rights

Fatema Gunja et al.

Fatema Gunja, Alexandra Cox, Marsha Rosenbaum, and Judith Appel contend in the following viewpoint that drug testing students before they can participate in extracurricular activities is not only ineffective but harmful. These activities are beneficial to students, the authors assert, yet students will not join because they do not wish to take a drug test. Drug testing also results in false positives, infringes on students' privacy and confidentiality rights, and implicitly accuses youth of using drugs, the authors argue. Fatema Gunja is director of the Drug Policy Forum of Massachusetts; Alexandra Cox and Judith Appel work in the Office of Legal Affairs for Drug Policy Alliance; and Marsha Rosenbaum is director of the Drug Policy Alliance of San Francisco.

As you read, consider the following questions:
1. According to the *Journal of School Health* study, what should effective alternatives to drug testing address?
2. Which state's supreme court found that random, suspicionless drug testing violates students' privacy?
3. Name three unintended negative consequences of random drug testing, as cited by the authors.

Fatema Gunja, Alexandra Cox, Marsha Rosenbaum, and Judith Appel, *Making Sense of Student Drug Testing: Why Educators Are Saying No.* American Civil Liberties Union–Drug Policy Litigation Project and Drug Policy Alliance, January 2004. Copyright © 2004 by the American Civil Liberties Union–Drug Policy Litigation Project and Drug Policy Alliance. Reproduced by permission.

The first large-scale national study on student drug testing found no difference in rates of drug use between schools that have drug testing programs and those that do not. Based on data collected between 1998 and 2001 from 76,000 students nationwide in 8th, 10th, and 12th grades, the study found that drug testing did not have an impact on illicit drug use among students, including athletes.

Dr. Lloyd D. Johnston, an author of the study, directs *Monitoring the Future*, the leading survey by the federal government of trends in student drug use and attitudes about drugs. According to Dr. Johnston, "[The study] suggests that there really isn't an impact from drug testing as practiced. . . . I don't think it brings about any constructive changes in their attitudes about drugs or their belief in the dangers associated with using them." Published in the April 2003 *Journal of School Health*, the study was conducted by researchers at the University of Michigan and funded in part by the National Institute on Drug Abuse.

The strongest predictor of student drug use, the study's authors note, is students' attitudes toward drug use and their perceptions of peer use. The authors recommend policies that address "these key values, attitudes, and perceptions" as effective alternatives to drug testing. The results of the national study are supported by numerous surveys and studies that examine the effectiveness of different options for the prevention of student drug misuse.

Set against the evidence from this national study and expert opinion, a handful of schools claim anecdotally that drug testing has reduced drug use. The only formal study to claim a reduction in drug use[1] was based on a snapshot of six schools and was suspended by the federal government for lack of sound methodology. . . .

Some States See Random Drug Testing as an Invasion of Privacy

In 2002, by a margin of 5 to 4, the U.S. Supreme Court permitted public school districts to drug test students participating in competitive, extracurricular activities in the case *Pot-*

1. a study conducted by Oregon Health and Science University in 2002

tawatomie v. Earls. In its ruling, however, the Court only interpreted *federal* law. Schools are also subject to *state* laws—which may provide greater protections for students' privacy rights. These laws vary greatly from state to state, and in many states, the law may not yet be well defined by the courts. For instance, random drug testing programs in Iowa are prohibited because the State Constitution forbids suspicionless searches of any kind. An Iowa school district's drug testing program, then, could still be challenged under state law.

School Officials and Parents Say No to Drug Testing

"[We stopped testing because] we didn't think it was the deterrent that we thought it would be . . . we didn't think it was as effective with the money we spent on it."

—*Scott Dahl, Vice President of*
School Board in Guymon, Oklahoma

"[We decided not to drug test because] it's really a parental responsibility . . . it is not our job to actually test [students]."

—*Harry M. Ward, Superintendent*
in Matthews County, Virginia

"The concerns of parents [in opposing a student drug testing proposal] have ranged from the budgetary issues to losing our focus on education to creating a threatening environment."

—*Laura Rowe, President of Band Aids, parent association*
of the HS band program in Oconomowoc, Wisconsin

"We object to the urine-testing policy as an unwarranted invasion of privacy. We want schools to teach our children to think critically, not to police them."

—*Hans York, Parent and Deputy*
Sheriff in Wahkiakum, Washington

"I would have liked to see healthy community participation that stimulates thoughtful interaction among us. Instead, this [drug testing] policy was steamrolled into place, powered by mob thinking."

—*Jackie Puccetti, Parent in El Paso, Texas*

In many states, including Arkansas, Indiana, Maryland, Michigan, Ohio, Oklahoma, Oregon, Texas, and Washington, lawsuits have been filed against school districts for their drug testing policies. Many of these school districts spend years and thousands of taxpayer dollars battling these law-suits with no guarantee of success.

U.S. Supreme Court *Did Not* Say . . .

• The Court *did not* say that schools are rquired to test students involved in competitive extracurricular activities.

• The Court *did not* say drug testing of all students or specific groups of students outside of those participating in competitive, extracurricular activities (i.e. student drivers) is constitutional.

• The Court *did not* say it is constitutional to drug test elementary school children.

• The Court *did not* say that it is constitutional to test by means other than urinalysis.

• The Court *did not* say that schools are protected from law-suits under their respective state laws.

In late 2003, the Supreme Court of Pennsylvania struck down the random, suspicionless drug testing of student participants in extracurricular activities and those with parking passes, finding that this program violated the heightened privacy protections provided by the Pennsylvania constitution.

Random Drug Testing Is a Barrier to Joining Extracurricular Activities

Random drug testing is typically directed at students who want to participate in extracurricular activities, including athletics. However, drug testing policies may prevent some students from engaging in these activities. Research shows the vastly disproportionate incidence of adolescent drug use and other dangerous behavior occurs during the unsupervised hours between the end of classes and parents' return home in the evening.

Research also shows that students who participate in extracurricular activities are:

• Less likely to develop substance abuse problems;
• Less likely to engage in other dangerous behavior such as violent crime; and
• More likely to stay in school, earn higher grades, and set —and achieve—more ambitious educational goals.

In addition, after school programs provide students who are experimenting with or misusing drugs with productive activities and contact with a teacher, coach, or even a peer who can help them identify and address problematic drug use.

One of many school districts facing lawsuits regarding privacy concerns and confidentiality, the Tulia Independent School District has seen a dramatic reduction in student participation in extracurricular activities since implementing drug testing. One female student explains:

"I know lots of kids who don't want to get into sports and stuff because they don't want to get drug tested. That's one of the reasons I'm not into any [activity]. Cause . . . I'm on medication, so I would always test positive, and then they would have to ask me about my medication, and I would be embarrassed. And what if I'm on my period? I would be too embarrassed."

Innocent Students Will Be Punished and Their Rights Will Be Violated

A positive drug test can be a devastating accusation for an innocent student. The most widely used drug screening method—urinalysis—will falsely identify some students as illicit drug users when they are not actually using illicit drugs at all, because drug testing does not necessarily distinguish between drug metabolites that have closely similar structures. For example:

- Over the counter decongestants may produce positive results for amphetamine.
- Codeine can produce a positive result for heroin.
- The consumption of food products with poppy seeds can produce a positive result for opiates.

When Tecumseh High School in Oklahoma enacted its random drug testing program, the school failed to ensure the protection of private information concerning prescription drug use submitted under the testing policy. The Choir teacher, for instance, looked at students' prescription drug lists and left them where other students could see them. The results of a positive test, too, were disseminated to as many as 13 faculty members at a time. Other students figured out the results when a student suddenly was suspended from his/her activity shortly after the administration of a drug test. This not only violates students' privacy rights, but can also lead to costly litigation.

In a desire to eliminate the possibility for false positives, schools often ask students to identify their prescription medications before taking a drug test. This both compromises students' privacy rights and creates an added burden for schools to ensure that students' private information is safely guarded.

Drug Testing May Worsen Substance Abuse Problems

Drug testing says very little about who is misusing or abusing drugs. Hundreds or even thousands of students might be tested in order to detect a tiny fraction of students who may have used the drugs covered by the test. Additionally, students misusing other harmful substances not detected by drug tests will not be identified. If schools rely on drug testing, they may undervalue better ways of detecting young people who are having problems with drugs. Most often, problematic drug use is discovered by learning to recognize its common symptoms. Teachers, coaches, and other school officials can identify students with a drug problem by paying attention to such signs as student absences, erratic behavior, changes in grades, and withdrawal from peers.

[As a result of drug testing,] students may turn to more dangerous drugs or binge drinking. Because marijuana is the most detectable drug, students may switch to drugs they think the test will not detect, like Ecstasy (MDMA) or inhalants. Knowing alcohol is less detectable, they may also engage in binge drinking, creating greater health and safety risks for students and the community as a whole. . . .

Students learn that they are guilty until proven innocent. Students are taught that under the U.S. Constitution, people are presumed innocent until proven guilty and that they have a reasonable expectation of privacy. Random drug testing undermines both lessons; students are assumed guilty until they can produce a clean urine sample, with little regard given to students' privacy rights.

"Drug and alcohol testing are effective and extremely accurate if properly administered and student dignity and privacy are preserved."

Random Drug Testing Is Necessary and Does Not Violate Students' Rights

David G. Evans

In the following viewpoint David G. Evans touts the effectiveness of random drug testing for students, calling it a strong weapon to fight drug use. He supports this view with studies that show students are less likely to use drugs when they know they may be tested. Accuracy of test results is ensured when a three-step process is followed, he contends. Furthermore, he asserts, federal laws protect students' privacy, and courts have upheld the constitutionality of testing students who participate in extracurricular activities. Evans dismisses charges that students will choose not to participate in school activities rather than take a required drug test. David G. Evans is executive director of the Drug-Free Schools Coalition.

As you read, consider the following questions:
1. According to the viewpoint, what were the results of random drug testing of athletes at an Oregon high school?
2. What are the provisions of the two laws that protect student confidentiality, according to Evans?
3. What is the author's response to arguments that students should not have to choose between their privacy and extracurricular activities required to get into college?

David G. Evans, "DSC Information Kit," www.studentdrugtesting.org, 2002. Copyright © 2002 by David G. Evans. Reproduced by permission.

Many schools find great value in using random drug and alcohol testing as part of their anti-drug programs. The goal of testing is to deter drug and alcohol use. Students who know they may be detected are less likely to use drugs or alcohol.

The courts clearly support testing when there is a reasonable suspicion that a student is under the influence in school. The courts also support random testing of student athletes and students who participate in extracurricular activities or drive on the school campus because these are privileges and schools can set conditions on participation.

Drug and alcohol testing are effective and extremely accurate if properly administered and student dignity and privacy are preserved. Some parents have concerns about testing. In most cases they do not understand how testing works and how accurate it is. Once it is explained to them, and they understand the protections built into a good testing process, their concerns are relieved. Most parents support testing. They recognize that student drug and alcohol use is often difficult to detect from observation alone.

The Checks and Balances in the Drug Testing Process

Drug testing in the workplace, in schools and in professional athletics is usually done by a three step process: (1) an initial screening test that if positive (2) is confirmed by an alternate technology [and] (3) [its] final results [are] reviewed by a Medical Review Officer (MRO), a physician trained in drug testing and substance abuse.

Drug testing begins with the collection of a urine, saliva or hair specimen. There are well-established procedures for collecting specimens. The chain of custody of the specimen must be protected. Chain of custody is the documentation of the specimen collection and then safe handling of the specimen from collection to analysis. Urine and saliva testing can be done on-site at a school or in a laboratory. Hair testing requires use of a laboratory.

Initial drug tests are generally confirmed by a process called gas chromatography/mass spectrometry (GC/MS). This process meets legal accuracy standards.

Positive results should be reviewed by a Medical Review Officer, a physician trained in evaluating drug tests results who will consult with the student and the student's parents if the test is positive to determine if the drug use was legitimate due to a doctor's prescription or illegitimate due to illegal drug use.

The results should be kept confidential and only released on a need to know basis. Confirmed positive drug test results can then be used to deny privileges and/or to initiate further evaluation of the student.

Studies on Student Random Drug Testing

Random drug testing gives schools a strong weapon to get drugs out of schools. School drug testing programs are a proven low cost method to win the fight for our children's future. Schools implementing drug testing experience a substantial reduction in drug use.

A recent study in Indiana schools by Joseph R. McKinney, J.D., Ed.D., Chair of the Department of Educational Leadership at Ball State University, demonstrates the effectiveness of student random drug testing. The question asked in the study was "Does the implementation of a random drug testing program result in a reduction of drug and alcohol use among high school students?" The study examined the effectiveness of a mandatory, random, suspicionless drug testing policy before and after court rulings. The Indiana Court of Appeals had ruled that student random drug testing was unconstitutional under the Indiana Constitution in August 2000. As a result, all Indiana schools halted their random drug testing programs in 2000. The Indiana Supreme Court reversed the lower court in 2002 and schools in Indiana have reinstated their programs [following the decision in] *Linke v. Northwestern School Corp.*

The study looked at high schools with random drug testing policies. Ninety-four high schools were identified. Of these schools, 83 high school principals responded to the survey. The principals were asked to contrast substance abuse activity during the 1999–2000 school year when drug testing policies were in effect with the 2000–2001 school year when schools were not permitted to use random drug testing. The results of the study are summarized below:

85% of the high school principals reported an increase in either drug usage or alcohol usage among their students after the drug testing program was stopped, compared to the school year when they had a drug testing plan implemented. 80% reported an increase in illicit drug usage. 59% reported an increase in alcohol usage.

83% reported their answers concerning the increase in drug and alcohol usage was based on information received directly from students. 79% said their answers were based on information from teachers and staff. 59% said information came from law enforcement. 23% said information came from formal surveys of students at the school.

78% of the principals reported that there was an increase (compared to the 1999–2000 year) in the number of students who came forward and told them that drug and alcohol usage was on the rise since the drug-testing program was stopped.

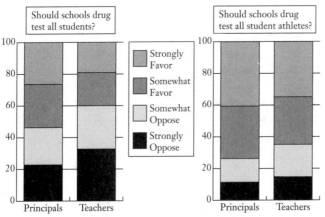

Opinions of 1,206 Middle School and High School Administrators on Student Drug Testing

Compiled by editor using data from CASA surveys of teachers, principals, teens, and parents, published by the National Center on Addiction and Substance Abuse at Columbia University, 1997.

The principals reported that 352 students were either suspended or expelled for drug- or alcohol-related incidents during the 1999–2000 school year but that during the 2000–2001 year (at the time they returned the survey, May 2001) without the drug-testing program that there were 518 drug- or alcohol-related suspensions/expulsions.

55% of the principals reported that coaches either indicated to them that they had received information that student athletes were involved in more incidents of drinking during the year without the drug-testing program. 57% reported the same regarding the use of drugs by student athletes. 97% of the drug testing programs included student athletes.

Studies Show That Random Testing Deters Drug Use

89% of the principals believe that the drug-testing program undermines the effects of peer pressure by providing a legitimate reason to refuse to use illegal drugs and alcohol.

Based on this data, random drug testing policies appear to provide a strong tool for schools to use in the battle to reduce alcohol and drug use among teens. Random drug testing has proven effective in decreasing drug use by students. Drug testing programs in other contexts has also enjoyed remarkable success.

A study by researchers at Oregon Health and Science University shows that student athletes subject to random drug testing at an Oregon high school were almost four times less likely to use drugs than student athletes at a demographically similar school who were not tested. The student responses to the study were anonymous.

The study compared Wahtonka High School, where all student athletes were subject to random testing, with Warrenton High School, a similar school where athletes were not tested. Of the athletes subject to the random testing at Wahtonka, 5.3 % said they were using illicit drugs by the end of the school year, compared to 19.4 % of the athletes at Warrenton. THIS IS A 73% REDUCTION IN DRUG USE. The athletes who were tested were also three times less likely to use performance-enhancing drugs such as steroids.

The study, conducted during the 1999–2000 school year, was published in the January 2003 issue of the *Journal of Adolescent Health*.

The Cost Effectiveness and Confidentiality of Student Drug Testing

Drug testing is cost effective with the average cost per student of $19 per year. The cost per test (lab fee) ranges from $10 to $148.50. The mean cost is $42 and the median is $21. Only a small percentage of the students need to be tested in order to make it effective. Drug testing by deterring drug use in the school also saves a lot of hidden costs, such as staff time, medical costs due to staff being assaulted by students, damage to school property due to vandalism, and insurance costs.

Any concern schools had about being able to pay for testing has now been solved because the recent federal Leave No Child Behind Act of 2001 permits schools to use federal education funds for student drug testing. Student drug testing is a specific program initiative listed in this landmark law. . . .

If we prevent young people from using drugs through the age of 18, the chance of their using drugs as adults is very small. Common sense tells us that preventing young people from experimenting with drugs in the first place is preferable to later and more costly treatment, rehabilitation and possible incarceration.

Student confidentiality is protected by two important federal laws. The first is the Family Educational Rights and Privacy Act which prohibits student records from being released, including drug and alcohol testing results, without the consent of the parents, or if the student is 18, without the student's consent. In addition, student treatment records are protected by the federal Confidentiality of Alcohol and Drug Abuse Patient Records regulations that carry federal criminal penalties for improperly releasing information.

Students Will Choose Extracurricular Activities over Drugs

The American Civil Liberties Union (ACLU) has criticized student drug testing because they claim that giving drug tests to students who participate in extracurricular activities will make the activities less attractive to students. They claim that [students who do not participate] in extracurricular activities . . . will choose to participate in drug-related behavior. While it is true that extracurricular activities help students to lead a positive life, there is no evidence that there is a drop off in participation because of drug testing. The ACLU could not present any such evidence to the U.S. Supreme Court. In fact, students report that drug testing gives them a reason to say "no" to drugs and still be "cool" with the other students. In a recent *Seventeen Magazine* poll, 54 percent of the young people said they would take a drug test "no problem." A *USA TODAY* poll showed that 70% of adults support testing of students in athletics and extracurricular activities.

We want students to make choices such as "do I smoke a joint or do I stay on the football team?" Our experience is that students choose the extracurricular activity over the drug. Some critics say that extracurricular activities are a requirement to get into college and students should not be forced to choose between extracurricular activities and their beliefs about their privacy. School-based extracurricular activities are not needed to get into college. There are many activities outside of school such as athletics, plays, competitions like chess clubs, or service work that can go on a college resume.

"School punishments greatly out of proportion to the offense arouse controversy by violating basic perceptions of fairness."

School Zero Tolerance Policies for Drugs Are Unjust

Russell J. Skiba

In the following viewpoint zero tolerance expert Russell J. Skiba argues that school policies that mandate severe punishment for drug possession or use infringe on students' rights. These zero tolerance policies often result in cruel and unusual punishment for trivial incidents, the author contends. Administrators violate students' due process rights, Skiba claims, by issuing harsh punishment without considering circumstances or students' past behavior. Russell J. Skiba is codirector of the Safe and Responsive Schools Project and associate professor in Counseling and Educational Psychology at Indiana University.

As you read, consider the following questions:

1. According to the viewpoint, what punishment did a high school senior receive for taking a sip of sangria at a luncheon during her internship?
2. What does the author say is not anomalous but inherent in the philosophy and application of zero tolerance policies?
3. In Skiba's contention, what seems to differentiate the most visible of zero tolerance cases?

Russell J. Skiba, "Zero Tolerance, Zero Evidence: An Analysis of School Disciplinary Practice," *Indiana Education Policy Center Report #SRS2*, August 2000. Copyright © 2000 by the Indiana Education Policy Center. Reproduced by permission.

Zero tolerance policies purposely increase the intensity of consequences for all offenders. Yet the practice of punishing relatively minor incidents harshly has been consistently controversial. Almost from the inception of a national zero tolerance drug policy, the harsh punishments meted out for relatively minor infractions raised a host of civil rights concerns: The American Civil Liberties Union considered filing suit on behalf of those whose automobiles, boats, and even bicycles had been impounded with trace amounts of marijuana. By 1990, the Customs Service boat impoundment program was quietly phased out after a Woods Hole Oceanographic Institute research vessel was seized for a marijuana cigarette found in a seaman's cabin.

Similar controversy has attended a host of suspensions and expulsions associated with zero tolerance for relatively trivial incidents in school settings. [A 1999 report by R.J.] Skiba and [R.L.] Peterson presented some of the suspensions and expulsions that received media attention from the passage of the Gun-Free Schools Act[1] in 1994 until May, 1998, including school expulsions for reasons ranging from paper clips to minor fighting to organic cough drops. This review updates that analysis, looking at cases of suspension or expulsion due to zero tolerance reported in the national newspapers from May, 1998 to December, 1999. The number of such cases appears, if anything, to be increasing, and a thorough description of all of those cases is certainly beyond the scope of this paper. The following is a representative sampling of such cases. . . .

Controversial Applications of Zero Tolerance

Although there is no federal mandate of suspension or expulsion for drug-related offenses, the application of zero tolerance to drugs or alcohol has become quite common. Again, the gravity of the events varies considerably.

• June, 1998, Brookline, Massachussetts: Nine seniors caught with alcohol on a bus going to their senior prom were barred by the principal from attending their gradua-

1. a national zero tolerance law that mandated expulsion for students carrying weapons but required schools to allow case-by-case review

tion, and two were not allowed to compete in the state baseball playoffs. Citing tragic accidents caused by alcohol abuse, Brookline High School Headmaster Robert Weintraub stated, "Every time there's a serious incident, a violation of drugs, alcohol, or weapons, I have taken a very hard line, because it's important for kids to get the message that if they do something that violates some of the fundamental rules we have here, they will be punished."

• June, 1998, Pinellas County, Florida: In their last month of school, two high school seniors skipped school and smoked marijuana with friends in the morning. School officials were tipped off and expelled the boys upon their arrival some hours later. A federal appeals court ruled against the district, however, stating that, in the absence of any actual drug test, the school had not "even a scintilla of evidence" that the two teens were under the influence at school.

• October, 1998, East Lake, Florida: High school senior Jennifer Coonce took a sip of sangria at a luncheon with co-workers as part of a school-sponsored internship. When her parents called the high school to complain about minors being served alcohol, the district suspended her for the remainder of the semester. Jennifer, an honors student, was offered the opportunity to take her college placement classes at home, over the telephone.

• February, 1999, Ewing, New Jersey: When a freshman dozed off in his social studies class, his teacher became suspicious he was using drugs and asked him to visit the school nurse for a check of his pulse and blood pressure. When the boy refused, the principal suspended him, and refused to readmit him until he had submitted to a drug test. Although the boy submitted to the test, his father considered filing a lawsuit challenging the policy.

Zero Tolerance Policies Are Irrational

The range of seriousness of these incidents, as compared with the relative consistency of punishment, may offer some insight into why zero tolerance creates controversy. A fairly stiff punishment for serious drinking or drug abuse at school-sponsored events seems fitting, and may well serve to prevent more serious harm. In contrast, the long-term suspension of

Zero Tolerance Isolates Youth Who Need Help

Instead of kicking kids out we should be lifting them up. Instead of more exclusion we should strive for greater inclusion, that is, invest in the creation of secure school environments where the kids with the greatest risk can receive the greatest assistance and range of resources, not the least, as is largely the case today.

The hard line of zero tolerance simply does not solve the problem of violence in our culture nor does it aid most other school problems such as adolescent drug use. According to numerous reviews, zero tolerance is a total failure, recapitulating our protracted, failed "war on drugs." The growing intolerance toward youth appears more to reflect blind ideology than enlightened leadership offering thoughtful and workable solutions to difficult social problems. . . .

Without the legal due process afforded adults, students in zero-tolerance high schools are increasingly being subjected to drug-sniffing dogs, warrantless locker and backpack searches, on-campus armed police, mandatory drug testing, and expulsion for possession or use, even when tests disclose weekend use off-campus. . . . Other than prisoners and felons on parole, few adults are subjected to this level of . . . scrutiny.

Aaron Kipnis, *Santa Barbara Independent*, February 2000.

---

an honors student for a sip of sangria seems more likely to turn the offender into the perceived victim, as the *St. Petersburg Times* notes in an editorial:

Zero tolerance policies are inherently unjust and irrational because they conflate harms. Accepting a cup of sangria for a good-bye toast is punished as severely as a student who gets drunk on school property. . . . Bringing a butter knife to school to cut an apple for lunch carries the same expulsion as toting a loaded magnum. Those harms are not equivalent, and if they are punished with equal severity, the system looks both unfair and nonsensical.

Strictures against cruel and unusual punishment are fundamental to our legal system. It may well be that school punishments greatly out of proportion to the offense arouse controversy by violating basic perceptions of fairness inherent in our system of law even when upheld by the courts. . . .

There is some tendency to assume that these suspensions or expulsions for trivial incidents are simply idiosyncratic or aberrations that occur in districts characterized by an over-zealous administration. Yet the ubiquity of these "trivial incidents" across time and location suggests that the over-extension of school sanctions to minor misbehavior is not anomalous, but rather is inherent in the philosophy and application of zero tolerance. School disciplinary data at both the district and national levels have shown that the serious infractions that are the primary target of zero tolerance (e.g., drugs, weapons, gangs) occur relatively infrequently. The most frequent disciplinary events with which schools wrestle are minor disruptive behaviors such as tardiness, class absence, disrespect, and noncompliance. A broad policy that seeks to punish both minor and major disciplinary events equally will, almost by definition, result in the punishment of a small percentage of serious infractions, and a much larger percentage of relatively minor misbehavior. We might expect then that the "trivial incidents" connected with zero tolerance will not abate, but may even accelerate as those policies continue to be extended by local districts.

Violation of Due Process Rights

In response, the number of lawsuits filed by parents in such incidents also appears to be increasing. The [2000] ruling of Judge Robert McLoskey against [six students in an] expulsion case is not unusual; in general, courts have tended to side with school districts in reviewing such cases, giving relatively broad leeway to district administrators in their interpretation of school disciplinary policy. Yet the courts have also begun to limit school district power in certain cases. In a case in Pennsylvania involving the expulsion of a 13 year old for using a Swiss Army knife as a nail-file, the court ruled against a school district's mandatory expulsion policy because it allowed no exceptions. In Costa Mesa, California, the 90 day suspension of a high school senior for a pipe found in his car by police officials off campus was overruled in court, since the action did not allow the student his due process right to present his side of the story. Thus far, such decisions appear to be based primarily on procedural grounds, for violations of district policy or state law, or for a failure to provide opportunities for required due process. What seems to differentiate the most visible of these cases is the unwillingness on the part of school boards and administrators to back down, regardless of parent or community pressure. Policymakers in these high profile incidents often claim that their "hands are tied," that they have little or no room for flexibility in the administration of district policy. It should be noted, however, that this intractability represents a local interpretation of zero tolerance that may go beyond the federal zero tolerance policy. Indeed, by requiring local districts to have in place a procedure allowing for case-by-case review, the Gun-Free Schools Act seems to mandate some degree of flexibility in the implementation of zero tolerance.

*"Boys and girls are entitled to be educated
in a drug-free school."*

School Zero Tolerance Policies
for Drugs Are Necessary

Patrick Tobin

In the following viewpoint Patrick Tobin asserts that drugs
and alcohol pose a major threat to students. Because students have the right to be educated in a drug-free school,
Tobin says, he and other British headteachers have implemented zero tolerance policies, much like those in American
schools. Zero tolerance calls for the automatic expulsion of
students who possess or sell drugs at school, he explains. Tobin warns that giving second chances to student drug users
is risky and argues that expulsion may help them to confront
their problem. Patrick Tobin has been a headteacher for
eighteen years and is vice chairman of the Headmasters' and
Headmistresses' Conference in Great Britain.

As you read, consider the following questions:
1. What two questions does the author raise about teen
   alcohol and drug use, based on the findings of the
   Report on Drugs and Alcohol?
2. In Tobin's opinion, parents appreciate a school that takes
   action as opposed to what?
3. Why is it risky to give a second chance to students
   caught using drugs, in the author's contention?

Patrick Tobin, "Schools Must Show Zero Tolerance over Alcohol and Drugs,"
Evening News (Edinburgh, Scotland), April 28, 1999. Copyright © 1999 by
Scotsman Publications, Ltd. Reproduced by permission of the author.

The Denver High School [Columbine] massacre, that cocktail of loveless youth, ghoulish fascination with evil, drug-sapped culture and dehumanisation via the Internet, offers a futuristic nightmare to the affluent society.

It is tempting to think that it could only happen in America.

But few who work in British schools would subscribe to such a delusion, aware as we are of the erosion of values in British society.

Shocking Survey Results

[In 1999] the Headmasters' and Headmistresses' Conference [HMC] published its *Report on Drugs and Alcohol*. Of boys and girls aged 14–15 in 20 HMC schools, nearly 30 per cent had experimented with illegal drugs regularly. It was small consolation that most contact with and use of drugs took place out of school.

The same is true of alcohol. In year ten [sophomore year] where by definition every 14 and 15-year-old boy and girl is breaking the law when purchasing alcohol, two-thirds of boys and three in five girls had drunk in the previous seven days. The most frequent location was home, most boys and girls claiming that their parents always knew. The most frequent place of purchase, however, was a pub or bar, followed in popularity by the off-licence [liquor store].

HMC day school heads generally saw alcohol as a more urgent threat than drugs. For me this raised two fundamental questions. In what sense can schools reasonably be expected to stem the tide which has relaxed licensing laws, marketed alcohol with unchecked ruthlessness and made Britain notorious throughout the civilised world as a nation of inebriated louts? And how can we expect teenagers to respect the law on drugs when they are allowed by parents and society to break the law on drink on a massive scale and with impunity for all? . . .

The Dangers of Drugs

Experts on psychopharmocology are damning about those who blithely say that cannabis poses little threat to health. Yes, most of the boys and girls who risk using it seem to emerge relatively unscathed, but a significant proportion do not.

In my experience as a headteacher, those involved with cannabis usually betray symptoms in their anti-social behaviour and in their withdrawal from personal responsibility. They are also, because it is illegal, involved in a particularly sordid business with evil and exploitative people. I perceive no evidence whatever that drug-taking leads to happiness.

Principals Support Zero Tolerance

We should not have to apologize for upholding our communities' expectations for safe, orderly, and drug-free schools [using zero tolerance policies]. . . .

All the studies by law enforcement agencies (including the FBI and Secret Service), think tank reports, safety summits, government decrees, and a minor industry that has developed around school safety, have yet to find [a better] way [to assure safety]. . . .

Support the outstanding women and men who are providing tireless and conscientious leadership to insure safe, orderly, and drug-free environments . . . ! The press and others make a case for students' rights. We too believe strongly in students' rights—[especially their] right to live!

Gerald N. Tirozzi and Vincent L. Ferrandino, *Education Week*, January 26, 2000.

The social costs of drugs are vast already. Half of all recorded crime is drug-related, along with a startlingly high proportion of road accidents. The estimated annual cost of dealing with people classified as drug abusers is well over $4 billion.

The HMC report on Drugs and Alcohol said: "We see no adequate grounds for legalising cannabis, and we believe the decriminalisation lobby is confusing to young people." Even if cannabis were legalised, most HMC members would fight to keep it out of their schools.

Schools That Take Action Are Appreciated

My policy as headteacher has been consistent. Anyone who brings drugs into school or who sells them to other pupils will automatically be expelled.

On this basis, I have four times had to expel small groups

of boys. To that extent, like most of the headteachers I know, I practise "zero tolerance".

In each instance, I have communicated openly with parents as a whole and I have always received strong affirmations of support. While few headteachers welcome the inevitable headline, "Top school rocked by drugs scandal", we know parents appreciate that the school which is not afraid to take action is always preferable to one which pretends the problem does not exist. Headteachers tend to get criticised when they expel. What is expulsion going to do for the adolescent in trouble? I know boys who have been expelled, who have gone on to other schools and who have put their problems behind them. One young man, years later, went out of his way to thank me for the way I had handled his problem. He clearly saw it as a check which he had needed to receive.

Ensuring That Students Remain Drug-Free

For a long time most of independent school headteachers whom I know have judged other types of involvement with drugs in the light of individual circumstances. We tend to give a second chance to someone who gives way to peer pressure and says "yes" when we would have wished him to say "no". That said, the second chance carries with it the element of risk to others. The casual drug-taker easily becomes the drug-pusher or, at least, the link in a pusher's chain.

Other boys and girls are entitled to be educated in a drug-free school. As one parent said to me the other day, while as a citizen he is offended when a boy is expelled, as a parent he is worried when that boy arrives in his own son's school.

It is likewise inevitable that parents will worry when boys or girls, known to have been involved with drugs, receive second chances in their original school. That is why many schools, ours included, are adopting random drugs testing for youngsters who are known to have used drugs.

These boys and girls accept that, at any time, the school can ask them to accept a drugs test. This offers reassurance to parents who have a right to expect that their children will not be rubbing shoulders with drug-takers. It also, by helping to rebuild trust, is a step towards real rehabilitation. We support this through home-school agreements which place restrictions on the youngster's out-of-home social activity.

Intelligent and Principled Education

Ultimately, the only antidote to drugs is good education—in school and in the home.

The young should receive teaching based on the unique value of each human being—teaching which promotes self-esteem, provides correct and authoritative information, and encourages boys and girls to look after their own wonderful bodies and minds and to avoid risk.

What they are entitled to is an intelligent and principled lead from those entrusted with their upbringing—parents, schools and politicians.

"There must be an end to . . . barriers to education for youth who have been directed into the criminal justice system and away from school."

Student Drug Offenders Should Have Access to Federal Financial Aid

Drug Policy Alliance

The Drug Policy Alliance advocates alternatives to the war on drugs. In this viewpoint the organization denounces drug policies that prevent students, especially nonwhites, from accessing higher education. A provision of the Higher Education Act (HEA), it explains, unfairly bars students who have been convicted of a misdemeanor or felony drug offense from receiving college financial aid. This law steers young drug users away from school, the group asserts. Moreover, the Drug Policy Alliance alleges, the proviso disproportionately affects nonwhites, who are more likely to be prosecuted for drug crimes than are whites.

As you read, consider the following questions:
1. According to the author, what is ironic about the war on drugs as it relates to youth?
2. How does the Drug Policy Alliance explain its claim that young Native Americans face harsher penalties for criminal conduct than do other youth?
3. In the author's contention, how do the HEA drug provision and other drug policies affect youths' access to opportunities, and ultimately, affect the civil rights movement?

Drug Policy Alliance, "Education vs. Incarceration," www.drugpolicyalliance.com, 2005. Copyright © 2005 by Drug Policy Alliance. Reproduced by permission.

"We are tracking one group of kids from kindergarten to prison, and we are tracking one group of kids from kindergarten to college."

—Lani Guinier

In the United States, youth of color caught in the crossfire of the war on drugs are frequently subject to persecution, incarcerated and denied access to education opportunities. The irony is that the war on drugs is often defended as a necessary policy to protect the nation's young people. In reality, rather than protecting youth, the drug war has resulted in the institutionalized persecution of Black, Latino and Native American young people. While more and more young men and women of color are being ushered into the criminal justice system under the guise of fighting drugs, resources for educating youth are diminishing and barriers to education restrict students with drug convictions from receiving higher education.

Youth of color bear the brunt of harmful drug policies, from arrest to prosecution to detention in correctional facilities. Some states in the U.S. now have the distinction of sending more Black and Latino young people to prison every year than graduate from state university programs. This legacy of discrimination in U.S. drug policy amplifies the burgeoning gap in opportunities available to White youth and youth of color. In order to correct this discrepancy, policies must be enacted that make education a priority over incarceration. There must be an end to drug laws whose effect is to criminalize youth of color, racially discriminatory policing practices and barriers to education for youth who have been directed into the criminal justice system and away from school.

The Justice System Targets Blacks, Latinos, and Native American Youth

Although White youth sell and use drugs at the same or higher rates as youth of color, Black and Latino youth are arrested, prosecuted and imprisoned at dramatically higher rates for drug crimes. In 1980, 14.5% of all juvenile drug arrests were Black youth; by 1990, Black youth constituted 48.8% of juvenile drug arrests. A Black youth with a drug case is more than twice as likely to be held in police custody for a drug offense than a White youth. While half of all drug arrests involving White youth result in formal processing, 75% of drug arrests involving Black youth are prosecuted. Among young people incarcerated in juvenile facilities for the first time on a drug charge, the rate of commitment among Black youth is 48 times that of Whites, while the rate for Latino youth is 13 times that of Whites. Black youth are three times more likely than White youth to be admitted to an adult prison for a drug conviction. While the rate of young Whites being sent to prison for drug offenses from 1986–1996 doubled, the comparable Black rate increased six-fold.

The HEA Drug Provision Punishes Students Twice for the Same Crime

These would-be students having their aid cut already paid whatever price the criminal justice system demands. It doesn't make sense to continually punish young people in such a way that limits their ability to get an education and improve their lives. Additionally, judges handling drug cases already have the option of denying drug offenders federal benefits, and school administrators have the power to expel problem students. These are the people who know the students best, and they should be the ones who decide their educational futures—not the federal government.

Raise Your Voice! The Coalition for Higher Education Act Reform, http://raiseyourvoice.com.

Because crimes committed on Indian reservations often fall within federal jurisdiction, Native American youth who engage in minor criminal conduct that ordinarily would be prosecuted in state court instead face federal prosecution and federal penalties that are often far harsher than those imposed in state court. For this reason, approximately 60% of youth in federal custody are Native American. Disabled children are also disadvantaged in the juvenile justice system because they may lose their statutory entitlement to individualized education programs upon being transferred to adult facilities.

Education, Not Incarceration

In the past decade, many U.S. states have cut their budgets for higher education funds to compensate for rapid growth in prison populations and prison construction, fueled in part by increasing numbers of drug offenders in state and federal prisons. In both New York and California, prison expenditures now exceed university financing and more Black men are admitted as prisoners than graduate from the state universities. From 1977–1995, the U.S. prison spending increased by 823% while spending on higher education went up by only 374%.

The drug provision of the Higher Education Act, passed in 1998 by the United States Congress, delays or denies federal financial aid for higher education for any student convicted of a misdemeanor or felony drug offense. Given the disproportionately high numbers of Black and Latino youth arrested, detained, prosecuted and convicted for drug offenses, this policy will have a disparate impact on the education of youth of color. In this way, the unequal access to opportunities—for education, employment and a decent life—between black and white youth is exacerbated and sustained, guaranteeing the perpetuation of racial disparities in their future lives as adults and in the lives of their children and grandchildren through the generations.

The rate at which minority youth are relegated to lives of incarceration and its consequences serves to negate many of the hard-fought gains of the civil rights movement. During the last half of the 20th century, Blacks and other minorities in the U.S. struggled to win the right to equal opportunity in employment, housing, education and public accommodations. These rights are meaningless to hundreds of thousands of minority prisoners and non-violent drug offenders. Because of the drug war Black and Latino communities in the U.S. have lost a generation of young men to the criminal justice system. Statistical projections suggest that future generations of minority males will be lost unless U.S. drug policies are reformed.

"It is shocking that anyone would object to this common-sense legislation."

Student Drug Offenders Do Not Deserve Federal Financial Aid

Joyce Nalepka

Joyce Nalepka in the following viewpoint praises Congressman Mark Souder for sponsoring a provision of the Higher Education Act that bars drug offenders from receiving federal financial aid for college until they undergo rehabilitation and drug tests. The author, referring to an incident in which Mr. Souder was harangued by five members of Students for Sensible Drug Policy (SSDP) at a financial aid seminar, says that the pro–drug legalization group is misguidedly complaining about a law that keeps campuses safe and free of dealers and addicts. Only those who obey the law deserve federal funds, she contends. Joyce Nalepka is president of Drug-Free Kids: America's Challenge.

As you read, consider the following questions:

1. According to Nalepka, what happens after students attend conferences to discuss legislation barring drug offenders from receiving loans?
2. By whom is Souder highly respected, according to the author?
3. In Nalepka's view, why is it important for families to prevent or stop their children's drug use before they go to college?

Joyce Nalepka, "Applaud Souder's Efforts to Fight Illegal Drug Use," *Journal Gazette*, March 21, 2002. Copyright © 2002 by Joyce D. Nalepka. Reproduced by permission.

The [February 2002] verbal attack on Rep. Mark Souder by the so-called Students for Sensible Drug Policy who traveled from Indiana, Illinois and Washington, D.C., to Fort Wayne [Indiana] was as senseless as is illegal drug use.

As a 24-year veteran in the effort to educate parents, students, teachers and voters about the damage done by marijuana and other drugs, I have encountered pro-drug legalization organizations all across America. Legalization groups operate under names like the Drug Policy Foundation, Drug Policy Alliance, Lindesmith Center, Marijuana Policy Project and The National Organization for the Reform of Marijuana Laws (NORML).

[After an investigation,] two former congressmen, one Republican and one Democrat, called NORML the militant organizational arm of the drug culture supported by the drug culture magazines, the drug paraphernalia industry and, to a certain extent, even the traffickers.

SSDP Targets Congressman Souder

We have watched . . . Students for Sensible Drug Policy [(SSDP) evolve] from groups that promote legalization and that operate under various titles but share many of the same members. Students are invited to conferences at various universities to "discuss legislation prohibiting student loans to those convicted of drug offenses." It appears that the young people are then recruited into the legalization movement.

As far as continuing to shadow the congressman [Souder], Carolyn Lunman, an SSDP member from George Washington University, Washington, D.C. said, "He'd better watch his back."

At its Web site—http://www.drcnet.org/wol/226.html—SSDP threatens to "keep an eye on Souder's events calendar and will be developing a strategy to have a greater presence in Souder's district." This fringe group claims only 2,000 votes can defeat Souder. His defeat would be a tremendous loss to the drug fight.

If you wonder how students finance their participation and air travel to these various conferences or meetings to harass elected officials who, in Souder's case, have the interest of both the kids and his constituents at heart, visit their pro-drug Web site.

Students for Sensible Drug Policy is a militant fringe of the drug legalization movement. As parents, we would treat membership in SSDP as firmly as we would treat drug use. Stop the behavior and resign from the group or pay your own tuition.

Souder's Common-Sense Legislation

Souder has been targeted by the legalizers specifically because he has been doing the right thing—making every effort to curb drug use in America. He is highly respected by those of us who have been in the trenches for years. He is highly respected by those congressmen and women on both sides of the political aisle who have banded together to target drugs at the national level. Souder was selected by his peers to co-chair the Speaker's Task Force for a Drug-Free America.

Congressman Souder's Defense of His Drug Provision

Students who receive taxpayer-subsidized aid to go to college should be held accountable to follow our drug laws. . . .

We have attempted to address drug use among other groups through both prevention and enforcement. Why not college students? . . .

[Most taxpayers would] like to hold students who receive taxpayer subsidies accountable for violating anti-narcotics laws.

Mark Souder, *Journal Gazette*, January 11, 2002.

The very bill that these "Sensible Students" are complaining about prohibits any student with an illegal drug conviction from receiving a federally subsidized student loan, unless the student passes two drug tests and undergoes drug treatment.[1] If the student tests clean and goes through a drug rehabilitation program, the student could re-qualify for federal student aid.

It is shocking that anyone would object to this common

---

1. As of late 2004, the law remains in place.

sense legislation, which serves two purposes—to keep drug dealers and drug addicts off our campuses, where they are known to contribute to crime and the drop-out rate, and ensure that federal dollars for student aid go only to the deserving, not to those who break the law.

Moreover, it gives families leverage to prevent or stop their children's drug use. At a recent meeting with parents whose sons and daughters died of overdose while at college, the most frequently heard statement was, "If your child is already involved in illegal drugs, don't send him off to college. It's like an open-air drug market and there is no supervision."

Keeping Campuses Safe

We urge Souder's constituents to applaud his efforts and keep sending him back to Congress. He is one of the select few who is unafraid to stand up to the drug pushers.

Would you want your child or grandchild to end up in a dorm room with a non-rehabilitated drug criminal? Thanks, Congressman Souder, for making our colleges safer, and for protecting our campuses against the scourge of drugs.

Periodical Bibliography

The following articles have been selected to supplement the diverse views presented in this chapter.

Barbara Behrendt	"Drug Offense Waiver Proposed for Schools," *St. Petersburg Times*, March 31, 2004.
Common Sense for Drug Policy	"Higher Education Act Reform." www.csdp.org.
Marc Fisher	"Zero Tolerance—For Mistakes or Second Chances," *Washington Post*, April 29, 2004.
Jake Ginsky	"Smoke a Joint, Lose Your Loan," MotherJones.com, May 18, 2000.
Dean Kuipers	"Less than Zero: The New Age of Intolerance," *LA Weekly*, July 18, 2001.
Ken Maguire	"Bush to Enforce Financial Aid Drug Law," Associated Press, April 17, 2001.
Joseph R. McKinney	"The Effectiveness and Legality of Random Drug Testing Policies." www.studentdrugtesting.org.
Michelle Norris	"The Case for Zero Tolerance," Peter Jennings interview with Sandra Feldman, ABCNEWS.com: Zero Tolerance, May 11, 2003. www.happyvalleyasylum.com.
Marsha Rosenbaum	"Random Student Drug Testing Is No Panacea," *Alcoholism & Drug Abuse Weekly*, April 12, 2004.
Rick Shefchik	"It's Time to Loosen Up School Rules," Knight Ridder/Tribune News Service, December 3, 2002.
Society Guardian	"Zero Tolerance Conceals Drug Use in Schools," February 3, 2003. http://society.guardian.co.uk.
Mark Souder	"Law Meant to Hold Students Accountable," *Journal Gazette*, January 11, 2002.
Jacob Sullum	"Let the Love Flow: Student Drug Testing," *Reason*, May 2004.
U.S. Department of Justice	*Board of Education of Independent School District No. 92 of Pottawatomie County v. Lindsay Earls*, 2001. www.usdoj.gov.
Ryoko Yamaguchi, Lloyd D. Johnston, and Patrick M. O'Malley	"Relationship Between Student Illicit Drug Use and School Drug-Testing Policies," *Journal of School Health*, April 2003.

For Further Discussion

Chapter 1

1. Rod Paige uses descriptive language and metaphor to herald the No Child Left Behind (NCLB) Act's potential to narrow the education gap between disadvantaged students and their peers. Stan Karp, on the other hand, uses stark terms to forecast the chaos he thinks will be caused by NCLB, arguing that proponents of the law use "high-sounding rhetoric" that is appealing but merely covers up the damage the act will inflict. Whose style do you find more convincing, and why?

2. George W. Bush defines affirmative action as a quota system and asserts that it is therefore illegal. Graciela Elizabeth Geyer acknowledges that quota systems are illegal but insists that affirmative action programs do not use quotas. Based on your reading of the two viewpoints, do you think that affirmative action programs are quota systems? Why or why not?

3. Ward Connerly of the American Civil Rights Institute, which advocates that racial preferences have no place in American life or law, insists that education is not a human right. The American Civil Liberties Union of Southern California maintains that laws must ensure that people of all races have equal access to education. Do you think that education is a right? Do you believe that race-based policies effectively ensure equality, or are they a form of discrimination? Explain your answers.

Chapter 2

1. Mathew D. Staver uses the federal guidelines for prayer in public schools as evidence that all students' religious rights are protected. Ellen Johnson claims that federal guidelines shield only religious students. With whom do you agree? Why?

2. David L. Martinson quotes numerous newspaper articles and textbooks to make his point that school threat codes infringe on the rights of the speaker. David L. Stader cites court cases to demonstrate that these policies are both constitutional and necessary to protect students and teachers. Which type of evidence do you find more convincing, and why?

3. The authors in this chapter detail several situations in which school officials may or may not censor expression. Under what circumstances do you think students' speech should be restricted? Explain.

Chapter 3

1. Mitchell L. Yell and Michael E. Rozalski say that random school searches may be conducted without suspicion of a crime or consent by the students involved. In random searches, school officials randomly choose which lockers or cars to investigate. In contrast, during targeted searches administrators search a particular student who is suspected of violating a rule; schools must first believe that the safety or order of the school may be threatened by student behavior. In what situations, if any, do you think a school would be reasonable in conducting random searches? When should schools implement targeted searches?

2. Tanya L. Green argues that school-based clinics treat students without notifying their parents, which violates parents' rights. Under what circumstances, if any, should parents be informed of their teens' reproductive health? Explain.

3. Sonia Mukhi and Kate McCormack are students while Viet D. Dinh is former assistant attorney general for the Office of Legal Policy and Johnny N. Williams is employed by the Department of Homeland Security. How do you think these authors' credentials may be coloring their arguments for and against educational provisions of the Patriot Act?

Chapter 4

1. David G. Evans believes that drug testing is beneficial because it forces students to choose between drugs and extracurricular activities, and generally students decide not to use drugs. Fatema Gunja, Alexandra Cox, Marsha Rosenbaum, and Judith Appel predict that students wishing to maintain their privacy will decline to participate in extracurricular activities rather than take a drug test. In their opinion, the choice is between extracurricular activities and *privacy*, not drugs. With which argument do you agree, and why? What effect do you think random drug testing has on students?

2. Patrick Tobin uses the example of the Columbine massacre and refers to personal experiences to show that zero tolerance policies are necessary to combat drugs in schools. To illustrate what he sees as the injustice of zero tolerance, Russell J. Skiba adopts a formal tone and cites examples publicized in the media. Whose style do you find more convincing? Explain why.

Organizations to Contact

The editors have compiled the following list of organizations concerned with the issues debated in this book. The descriptions are derived from materials provided by the organizations. All have publications or information available for interested readers. The list was compiled on the date of publication of the present volume; the information provided here may change. Be aware that many organizations take several weeks or longer to respond to inquiries, so allow as much time as possible.

Advocates for Youth
2000 M St. NW, Suite 750, Washington, DC 20036
(202) 419-3420 • fax: (202) 419-1448
e-mail: questions@advocatesforyouth.org
Web site: www.advocatesforyouth.org

Advocates for Youth believes young people should have access to information and services that help prevent teen pregnancy and the spread of sexually transmitted diseases, and enable youth to make healthy decisions about sexuality. The organization publishes brochures, fact sheets, and bibliographies on adolescent pregnancy and sexuality, adolescent rights, and sexuality education.

American Civil Liberties Union (ACLU)
125 Broad St., Eighteenth Floor, New York, NY 10004-2400
(212) 549-2500
e-mail: aclu@aclu.org • Web site: www.aclu.org

The ACLU is a national organization that works to defend Americans' civil rights guaranteed by the U.S. Constitution. Seeking to protect the rights of students and others, it opposes random school searches, zero tolerance policies, campus speech codes, and certain provisions of the Patriot Act. The ACLU offers policy statements, pamphlets, its *Student Organizing Manual*, and the semiannual newsletter *Civil Liberties Alert*.

Americans United for Separation of Church and State (AUSCS)
518 C St. NE, Washington, DC 20002
(202) 466-3234 • fax: (202) 466-2587
e-mail: americansunited@au.org • Web site: www.au.org

Through litigation, education, and advocacy, AUSCS works to protect religious freedom for all Americans. It opposes the passing of federal or state laws that threaten the separation of church and state.

It prints brochures, pamphlets, and the monthly newsletter *Church and State*.

Center for Equal Opportunity (CEO)
14 Pidgeon Hill Dr., Suite 500, Sterling, VA 20165
(703) 421-5443 • fax: (703) 421-6401
e-mail: comment@ceousa.org • Web site: www.ceousa.org
The Center for Equal Opportunity is the only think tank devoted exclusively to the promotion of colorblind equal opportunity and racial harmony. CEO sponsors conferences, supports research, and publishes policy briefs on issues related to race, ethnicity, assimilation, and public policy. *Not a Close Question: Preferences in University Admissions* is one of its titles.

Center for the Prevention of School Violence (CPSV)
1801 Mail Service Center, Raleigh, NC 27699
(800) 299-6054 • (919) 733-3388 ext. 332
e-mail: jaclyn.myers@ncmail.net • Web site: www.cpsv.org
The CPSV is a primary point of contact for information, programs, and research about school violence and its prevention. As a clearinghouse, it provides information about all aspects of the problems that fall under the heading of school violence as well as information about strategies directed at solving these problems.

Concerned Women for America (CWA)
1015 Fifteenth St. NW, Suite 1100, Washington, DC 20005
(202) 488-7000 • fax: (202) 488-0806
e-mail: mail@cwfa.org • Web site: www.cwfa.org
CWA's purpose is to preserve, protect, and promote traditional Judeo-Christian values through education, legislative action, and other activities. It is concerned with creating an environment that is conducive to building strong families and raising healthy children. CWA publishes the monthly *Family Voice*, which prints articles that support school zero tolerance policies and mandatory parental involvement in children's reproductive health.

Drug Policy Alliance
925 Fifteenth St. NW, Second Floor, Washington, DC 20005
(202) 216-0035 • fax: (202) 216-0803
e-mail: dc@drugpolicy.org
Web site: www.drugpolicyalliance.org
The Drug Policy Alliance is dedicated to studying alternatives to the war on drugs. It supports legalization of drug use, though not for minors, as well as the repeal of the drug provision of the Higher Education Act. It publishes the quarterly *Drug Policy Letter*.

Eagle Forum

PO Box 618, Alton, IL 62002

(618) 462-5415 • fax: (618) 462-8909

e-mail: eagle@eagleforum.org • Web site: www.eagleforum.org

Eagle Forum is a Christian group that promotes morality and traditional family values as revealed through the Bible. It opposes the No Child Left Behind Act and college tuition subsidies for illegal immigrants. The forum publishes the monthly *Phyllis Schlafly Report* and a periodic newsletter.

Education World

1062 Barnes Rd., Suite 301, Wallingford, CT 06492

e-mail: webmaster@educationworld.com

Web site: www.educationworld.com

Education World is a site where teachers and administrators share ideas, find research materials, and read daily columns. Educators can browse hundreds of articles written by education experts and covering topics such as the No Child Left Behind Act, dress codes, and school safety. It prints *Education World Newsletter* and *Administrator's Desk Newsletter* weekly.

Family Research Council

801 G St. NW, Washington, DC 20001

(202) 393-2100 • fax: (202) 393-2134

e-mail: corrdept@frc.org • Web site: www.frc.org

The council seeks to promote and protect the interests of the traditional family. It focuses on issues such as parental autonomy and responsibility, community support for single parents, and adolescent pregnancy. Among the council's numerous publications are the papers "Ten Ways to Pray in Public Schools," and "Abstinence Until Marriage: The Best Message for Teens."

Freechild Project

PO Box 6185, Olympia, WA 98507

(360) 753-2686

e-mail: info@freechild.org • Web site: www.freechild.org

The Freechild Project is a think tank, resource agency, and advocacy group for young people around the world who seek to play a larger role in their schools and communities. Training and conferences are offered to help parents, teachers, and community leaders involve youth in their communities. The Freechild Project's students' rights directory, which offers a wealth of information about school uniforms, zero tolerance, free speech, and student equality, can be accessed on the Web site, along with booklets, fact sheets, speeches, and book reviews.

National Coalition Against Censorship (NCAC)
275 Seventh Ave., New York, NY 10001
(212) 807-6222 • fax: (212) 807-6245
e-mail: ncac@ncac.org • Web site: www.ncac.org

NCAC is an alliance of organizations committed to defending freedom of thought, inquiry, and expression by engaging in public education and advocacy on national and local levels. Its Web site contains a section on student rights. NCAC publishes periodic reports and the quarterly *Censorship News*.

National Education Association (NEA)
1201 Sixteenth St. NW, Washington, DC 20036
(202) 833-4000 • fax: (202) 822-7974
Web site: www.nea.org

NEA is America's oldest and largest volunteer-based organization dedicated to advancing the cause of public education. Its commitments at the local, state, and national levels include conducting workshops for teachers, lobbying for needed school resources and higher educational standards, and spearheading innovative projects that reshape the learning process. Two of NEA's publications, the monthly magazine *NEA Today Online* and biannual report *Thoughts and Action*, are available on its Web site.

Office of National Drug Control Policy (ONDCP)
Drug Policy Information Clearinghouse
PO Box 6000, Rockville, MD 20849-6000
(800) 666-3332 • fax: (301) 519-5212
e-mail: ondcp@ncjrs.org
Web site: www.whitehousedrugpolicy.gov

The Office of National Drug Control Policy formulates the government's national drug strategy and the president's antidrug policy. Its goals are to reduce illicit drug use, manufacturing, and trafficking, drug-related crime and violence, and drug-related health consequences. Its reports include *What You Need to Know About Drug Testing in Schools* and *The Challenge in Higher Education: Confronting and Reducing Substance Abuse on Campus*.

People for the American Way (PFAW)
2000 M St. NW, Suite 400, Washington, DC 20036
(202) 467-4999
e-mail: pfaw@pfaw.org • Web site: www.pfaw.org

PFAW is committed to reaffirming the traditional American values of pluralism, diversity, and freedom of expression and religion in many areas, including education. It is engaged in a mass media campaign to create a climate of tolerance and respect for diverse people, religions, and values. PFAW distributes educational materials, leaflets, and brochures and publishes the annual *Attacks on the Freedom to Learn.*

Student Press Law Center

1815 N. Fort Meyer Dr., Suite 900, Arlington, VA 22209
(703) 807-1904
Web site: www.splc.org

An advocate for student free-press rights, the SPLC provides information, advice, and legal assistance to students and educators in their struggle to discuss important issues free from censorship. It operates a formal Attorney Referral Network of approximately 150 lawyers across the country who are available to provide free legal representation to students. The *SPLC Report* is printed three times a year.

Students for Sensible Drug Policy (SSDP)

1623 Connecticut Ave. NW, Third Floor, Washington, DC 20009
(202) 293-4414 • fax: (202) 293-8344
e-mail: ssdp@ssdp.org • Web site: www.ssdp.org

Students for Sensible Drug Policy is committed to providing education on harms caused by the War on Drugs, working to involve youth in the political process, and promoting an open, honest, and rational discussion of alternative solutions to our nation's drug problems. SSDP prints pamphlets and flyers to encourage others to oppose drug testing in schools and to help repeal the drug provision of the Higher Education Act.

Bibliography of Books

| The Advancement Project and The Civil Rights Project | *Opportunities Suspended: The Devastating Consequences of Zero Tolerance and School Discipline Policies.* Cambridge, MA: Harvard University, 2000. |

Advisory Committee on Student Financial Assistance — *Empty Promises: The Myth of College Access in America.* Washington, DC: Advisory Committee on Student Financial Assistance, 2002.

Anti-Defamation League — *Responding to Bigotry and Intergroup Strife on Campus: Guide for College and University Presidents and Senior Administrators.* New York: Anti-Defamation League, 2001.

Kirk A. Bailey and Catherine J. Ross — *School Safety & Youth Violence: A Legal Primer.* Washington, DC: George Washington University, 2001.

Peter D. Blauvelt — *Making Schools Safe for Students.* Thousand Oaks, CA: Corwin Press, July 2000.

Michael Bochenek and A. Widney Brown — *Hatred in the Hallways: Violence and Discrimination Against Lesbian, Gay, Bisexual, and Transgender Students in U.S. Schools.* New York: Human Rights Watch, 2001.

William C. Bosher Jr., Kate R. Kaminski, and Richard S. Vacca — *The School Law Handbook: What Every Leader Needs to Know.* Alexandria, VA: Association for Supervision and Curriculum Development, 2004.

Tammy Bruce — *The New Thought Police: Inside the Left's Assault on Free Speech and Free Minds.* Roseville, CA: Forum, 2001.

Center for Mental Health in Schools at UCLA — *Introductory Packet on Violence Prevention and Safe Schools.* Los Angeles: UCLA Department of Psychology, 2004.

Kathleen Conn — *The Internet and the Law: What Educators Need to Know.* Alexandria, VA: Association for Supervision and Curriculum Development, 2002.

Alan M. Dershowitz — *Shouting Fire: Civil Liberties in a Turbulent Age.* Boston: Little, Brown, 2002.

Adam Fletcher — *Meaningful Student Involvement: Guide to Inclusive School Change.* Olympia, WA: The Freechild Project, 2003.

David A. French, Greg Lukianoff, and Harvey A. Silverglate — *Guide to Free Speech on Campus.* Philadelphia: Foundation for Individual Rights in Education, Inc., 2004.

Charles Haynes et al.   *The First Amendment in Schools.* Alexandria, VA:
                         Association for Supervision and Curriculum
                         Development, 2003.

Patricia H. Hinchey   *Student Rights: A Reference Handbook.* Santa Bar-
                         bara, CA: ABC-CLIO, 2001.

David L. Hudson Jr.   *The Silencing of Student Voices: Preserving Free
                         Speech in American Schools.* Nashville, TN: First
                         Amendment Center, 2004.

Peter Irons, ed.   *May It Please the Court: Courts, Kids, and the Con-
                         stitution.* New York: New Press, 2000.

John W. Johnson   *The Struggle for Student Rights: Tinker vs. Des
                         Moines and the 1960s.* Lawrence: University
                         Press of Kansas, 1997.

Office of National   *What You Need to Know About Drug Testing in
Drug Control Policy   Schools.* Washington, DC: Office of National
                         Drug Control Policy, 2002.

Ellen Frankel Paul   *The Right to Privacy.* New York: Cambridge
                         University Press, 2000.

Jamin B. Raskin   *We the Students: Supreme Court Decisions for and
                         About Students.* Washington, DC: CQ Press,
                         2003.

Frank S. Ravitch   *School Prayer and Discrimination: The Civil Rights
                         of Religious Minorities and Dissenters.* Boston:
                         Northeastern University Press, 1999.

Safe and Drug-Free   *Creating Safe and Drug-Free Schools: An Action
Schools Program and   Guide.* Washington, DC: U.S. Department of
Office of Juvenile   Education and U.S. Department of Justice,
Justice and Delinquency 1996.
Prevention

Kevin Saunders   *Saving Our Children from the First Amendment.*
                         New York: New York University Press, 2003.

Harvey A. Silverglate   *Guide to Due Process and Fair Procedure on
and Josh Gewolb   Campus.* Philadelphia: Foundation for Individ-
                         ual Rights in Education, 2004.

Thomas Sowell   *Affirmative Action Around the World: An Empiri-
                         cal Study.* New Haven, CT: Yale University
                         Press, 2004.

Abigail Thernstrom   *No Excuses: Closing the Racial Gap in Learning.*
and Stephan   New York: Simon & Schuster, 2003.
Thernstrom

Traci Truly   *Teen Rights: A Legal Guide for Teens and the
                         Adults in Their Lives.* Naperville, IL: Sphinx,
                         2002.

Index